Corrie ten Boom

Each New Day

Published by
World Wide Publications
1303 Hennepin Avenue
Minneapolis, Minnesota 55403

Scripture quotations in this volume identified KJV are based on the King James Version of the Bible.

Scripture quotations identified LB are from the Living Bible, Copyright © 1971 by Tyndale House Publishers, Wheaton, Illinois 60187. All rights reserved.

Scripture quotations from the Gospels identified Phillips are from THE NEW TESTAMENT IN MODERN ENGLISH (Revised Edition), translated by J. B. Phillips. © J. B. Phillips 1958, 1960, 1972. Used by permission of Macmillan Publishing Co., Inc.

Scripture quotations from the Epistles identified Phillips are from LETTERS TO YOUNG CHURCHES by J. B. Phillips. Copyright © 1947, 1957 by Macmillan Publishing Co., Inc., renewed 1975 by J. B. Phillips. Copyright © 1968 by J. B. Phillips. Used by permission.

Scripture quotations identified RSV are from the Revised Standard Version of the Bible, copyrighted 1946, 1952, © 1971 and 1973.

Library of Congress Cataloging in Publication Data

Ten Boom, Corrie.
   Each new day.

   1. Devotional calendars. I. Title.
BV4811.T4   242'.2   77-12780
ISBN 0-8007-0894-6

PREFACE

Here's a short daily message from me, Corrie ten
Boom, for *Each New Day.* There is something from
God's Word for every day. Some words may be of
greater impact for you than others, but you should
listen every day to what the Holy Spirit wants to say
to you through the message. A person is either a missionary or a mission field. Sometimes I wrote for
Christians who know that they are called to be the
light of the world. On other days God gave me a message about what it means to come to Him.

What about asking yourself some questions after
you have read the short remark, text, and prayer:

Did this message speak to me today?

Why?

How can I apply what the Lord was saying to me
in my circumstances?

Will it cost me something in my home, my work,
my church, or society?

Does it mean reconciliation, restitution, even
tribulation?

I know that the Lord gave me these words. They
are from Him who loves you and who spoke through
me to you.

Corrie ten Boom

BY CORRIE TEN BOOM WITH JAMIE BUCKINGHAM
Tramp for the Lord

BY CORRIE TEN BOOM WITH C.C. CARLSON
In My Father's House

BY CORRIE TEN BOOM WITH JOHN AND ELIZABETH SHERRILL
The Hiding Place

BY CORRIE TEN BOOM
Corrie's Christmas Memories
Corrie ten Boom's Prison Letters
He Cares, He Comforts—JESUS IS VICTOR
Each New Day

JANUARY

January 1

> May a dying Saviour's love
> And a risen Saviour's power
> And an ascended Saviour's prayer
> And a returning Saviour's glory
> Be the comfort and joy of your heart.

In our home in Haarlem, Holland, Father used to read Psalm 91 from the Bible and pray the very moment the first of January began. We consciously went into the new year together with the Lord. Do you fear the possibilities of this new year? Do as he did. Trust the Lord that in these coming days He will be your hiding place.

> He who dwells in the shelter of the Most High,
>   who abides in the shadow of the Almighty,
> will say to the Lord, "My refuge and my fortress;
>   my God, in whom I trust."
>
> Psalms 91:1, 2 RSV

Thank You, Lord Jesus, that You will be our hiding place, whatever happens.

January 2

May I give you something to do for the new year? Go alone before the Lord, and together with Him, examine yourself. Do you know that you are forgiven? Have you forgiven others? When you do that, God will give you a victorious new year.

(You) have put on the new nature, which is being renewed in knowledge after the image of its creator.

Colossians 3:10 RSV

Lord Jesus, at the start of this new year, we ask for a fresh beginning. Wipe our sins away with Your precious blood. Cleanse our hearts of bitterness toward others. Help us to live each new day in close communion with You, our true and faithful guide.

January 3

Jesus is Victor. Calvary is the place of victory. Obedience is the pathway of victory, Bible study and prayer the preparation. Courage, faith, the spirit of victory—every temptation is a chance for victory, a signal to fly the flag of our Victor, a chance to make the tempter know anew that he is defeated. Roy Hession writes in Calvary Road: "Jesus is always victorious. We have only to keep the right relationship with Him and His victorious life will flow through us and touch other people."

Put on the whole armour of God. . . .

Ephesians 6:11 KJV

Thank You, Lord Jesus, that You have won the victory for us.

January 4

"How can I nourish the life abundant?"

The Lord will show you. Be patient and wait for direction. In the meantime, read the Bible, meet with other children of God to pray together. Prayer fellowship is vital for your health as a Christian, and to accomplish God's work. Talk much with your Saviour. He knows, He loves, He cares.

Pray constantly.

1 Thessalonians 5:17 RSV

Lord, teach us to pray.

January 5

It is dark in the world. The mist is getting thicker and thicker. Where there is no vision, the people perish. The Lord is not willing to keep us in the dark, but wants to guide us with His victorious light.

> We are asking God that you may see things, as it were, from His point of view by being given spiritual insight and understanding. We also pray that your outward lives, which men see, may bring credit to your Master's Name, and that you may bring joy to His heart by bearing genuine Christian fruit, and that your knowledge of God may grow yet deeper.
>
> **Colossians 1:9, 10 Phillips**

Lord, what a comfort that Your insight and vision are perfect. Please help me to see things from Your point of view.

January 6

> God chose this world to be the arena of His plan, the center of what He has set Himself to do.
>
> **Watchman Nee**

> For God has allowed us to know the secret of His Plan, and it is this: He purposes in His sovereign will that all human history shall be consummated in Christ, that everything that exists in Heaven or earth shall find its perfection and fulfilment in Him. And here is the staggering thing—that in all which

will one day belong to Him we have been promised a share. . . .

Ephesians 1:9-11 Phillips

Lord, what a comfort it is to see Your perfect blueprint of this world. Thank You for making Your plan clear to us while we live in the midst of the chaos of today.

January 7

It has been said that the removal of small stones which frequently encumber the fields does not always increase the crop. In many soils they are an advantage, attracting the moisture and radiating the heat. In an experiment the results of removing the stones were so unfavorable to the crop that they were brought back again. We often cry to God, as Paul did, for the removal of some thorn in the flesh. Later experience teaches us that it was better for it to remain.

For the sake of Christ, then, I am content with weaknesses, insults, hardships, persecutions, and calamities; for when I am weak, then I am strong.

2 Corinthains 12:10 RSV

Your strength, my weakness—here they
    always meet,
When I lay down my burden at Your feet:
The things that seem to crush will in the end
Be seen as rungs on which I did ascend!
    Thank You, Lord.

January 8

God is voting for us all the time. The devil is voting against us all the time. The way we vote carries the election.

Choose you this day whom ye will serve . . . but as
for me and my house, we will serve the Lord.

Joshua 24:15 KJV

Yes, Lord, I again, or for the first time, choose
to be Yours. What joy to know that You chose me.
I lay my weak hand in Your strong hand. Together
with You, I am more than conqueror.

January 9

William Nagenda, the African evangelist, said:
"My life is like this ball bouncing on the floor. Sometimes the devil gives me a blow downwards, but
at the deepest spot Jesus is there, and He gives
me a blow upwards so that I come up higher than
I was before."

My soul clings to thee;
thy right hand upholds me.

Psalms 63:8 RSV

Lord, the devil is stronger than I am. But I know
from the Bible that You are much stronger than
the devil, and together with You I am much stronger
than the devil. Thank You, Lord, for that encouragement.

January 10

William Nagenda continued: "One day the devil
will give William a blow downwards so strong that
he will go all the way to the valley of the shadow
of death. There Jesus will give William a blow upwards so strong that he will come into heaven. The
devil will say, 'Where is William? I don't see him
anymore!' "

Even though I walk through the valley
of the shadow of death,

> I fear no evil;
> for thou art with me. . . .
>
> Psalms 23:4 RSV

Lord Jesus, thank You that You have overcome the forces of evil. We know that You will never let us down.

January 11

In my late teens I was fortunate to hear Sadhu Sundar Singh speak about his experiences of actually seeing the Lord.

When I met him during a walk, I told him of a worry I had. "Is there something wrong with my faith?" I asked. "I know that the Lord is with me, but I have never seen a vision or a miracle."

The Sadhu answered, "That I know Jesus is alive is no miracle—I have seen Him. But you, who have never seen Him, know His presence. Isn't that a miracle of the Holy Spirit?"

> Without having seen him you love him; though you do not now see him you believe in him and rejoice with unutterable and exalted joy.
>
> 1 Peter 1:8 RSV

Lord, we thank You that the Holy Spirit moves us to believe beyond our inadequate senses.

January 12

We must mirror God's love in the midst of a world full of hatred. A mirror does not do much. It only hangs in the right direction and reflects the light. We are mirrors of God's love, so we may show Jesus by our lives. He uses us to spread the Gospel of the Kingdom and to glorify Jesus.

But we all, with open face beholding as in a glass the glory of the Lord, are changed into the same image from glory to glory, even as by the Spirit of the Lord.

2 Corinthians 3:18 KJV

Thank You, Lord, that by Your Holy Spirit You turn our eyes in the right direction, looking unto You, that You can make us Your mirrors. What an honor, what a joy!

January 13

Open our eyes, dear Lord,
That we may see
The far vast reaches of eternity,
Help us to look beyond life's little cares
So prone to fret us
And the grief that wears
Our courage thin.
O may we tune our hearts
To Thy great harmony
That all the parts may ever be
In perfect, sweet accord.
Give us Thine own clear vision, blessed Lord.

Where there is no vision, the people perish.

Proverbs 29:18 KJV

Lord Jesus, it is only possible to have a view of unseen things through You. Thank You that You are willing to give it to us.

January 14

Can you do the things Jesus does? Can I? Yes! Because Jesus went to the Father, and there with His Father, He does greater things than He did when He was in the world. He does them through you and me.

I assure you that the man who believes in me will do the same things that I have done, yes, and he will do even greater things than these, for I am going away to the Father.

John 14:12 Phillips

Lord Jesus, thank You that You are willing to work through us. What a tremendous privilege!

January 15

Who is he who overcomes the world but he who believes that Jesus is the Son of God? The Lord is conqueror, and is able to hold you up and cause you to triumph in all situations. This has tremendously comforted me, even in the overwhelmingly difficult time when I was in prison.

He will keep you steadfast in the faith to the end, so that when His Day comes you need fear no condemnation.

1 Corinthians 1:8 Phillips

Thank You, Lord Jesus, for understanding our weakness and for giving us comfort, guidance, and power today and always.

January 16

We possess a divine artillery which silences the enemy and inflicts upon him the damage he would inflict on us.

As you live this new life, we pray that you will be strengthened from God's boundless resources, so that you will find yourselves able to pass through any experience and endure it with courage.

Colossians 1:11 Phillips

Lord, what joy to know that Your powers are so much greater than those of the enemy.

January 17

Arthur T. Pierson says in *God and Missions Today:* "The whole church of God should be a great body of evangelists. Instead of first absorbing pastor after pastor and then like insatiate sponges demanding ministrations of evangelists besides, church members should say to their minister, 'Let us alone and go after the lost.'"

> Ready to suffer grief and pain,
> Ready to stand the test.
> Ready to stay at home and send others
> If He sees best.
>
> Ready to go,
> Ready to stay,
> Ready my place to fill.
> Ready for service lowly or great,
> Ready to do His will.
>
> Ready to go,
> Ready to bear,
> Ready to watch and pray.
> Ready to stand aside and wait
> 'Til He shall clear the way.
>
> Ready to speak,
> Ready to think,
> Ready with heart and brain.
> Ready to stand where He sees fit.
> Ready to bear the strain.
>
> Ready to speak,
> Ready to warn,
> Ready o'er souls to yearn.
> Ready in life,
> Ready in death,
> Ready for His return.

> Go therefore and make disciples of all nations. . . .
>
> Matthew 28:19 RSV

My answer is yes, Lord Jesus, I mean it.

January 18

> Oh, to have one's soul as a field under heavenly cultivation; no wilderness, but a garden of the Lord. Walled around by grace, planted by instruction, visited by love, weeded by heavenly discipline, guarded by divine power. One's soul thus favored is prepared to yield fruit unto the glory of God.
>
> C. H. Spurgeon

> Until the Spirit is poured upon us from on high, and the wilderness becomes a fruitful field, and the fruitful field is deemed a forest.
>
> Isaiah 32:15 RSV

Father, make me Your garden. Prepare me to bring forth fruit to Your glory.

January 19

> You and I are what we are through the grace of God. The Christian life starts with grace, it must continue with grace, it ends with grace.

> The grace of the Lord like a fathomless sea,
> Sufficient for you, sufficient for me,
> Is tender and gracious and boundless and free,
> Sufficient for every need.

> For the grace of God has appeared for the salvation of all men.
>
> Titus 2:11 RSV

Lord, Thank You for Your ocean of love and grace.

January 20

I once saw a church that was really no more than a ceiling—here it was canvas, there it was metal. The people told me that once thay had a beautiful brick church, but they were in a country where Christianity was not allowed, and someone burned down the church.

I told them that I was so sorry they had lost their building, but they smiled. "God does not make mistakes. Some time ago," they said, "there was an earthquake on a Sunday morning. A thousand people were under this ceiling. Had we been in a brick building, many would have been injured, but this ceiling just quaked along with the earthquake, and no one was hurt."

> We know that in everything God works for good with those who love him, who are called according to his purpose.
>
> Romans 8:28 RSV

O Lord, thank You that Your side of the embroidery of our life is always perfect. That is such a comfort when our side is sometimes so mixed up.

January 21

Many times I have been guarded by divine power. Once when I was a prisoner, I was brought to a judge who asked me many questions. There was a possibility that I would be shot! After he had asked me many things, I said to him, "May I ask you something?"

"Go ahead," he said.

"Is there darkness in your life, or light?"

"Only darkness."

I told him the way of salvation. My sister, Betsie,

was questioned by the same judge, and she, too, brought him the Gospel. She even asked him if he would allow her to pray with him. He told me later, "I will never in my life forget your sister's prayers." Finally the Lord touched his heart, and he became our friend.

> Be not overcome of evil, but overcome evil with good.
>
> Romans 12:21 KJV

Lord, thank You that You are willing to guard me also, with Your divine power.

January 22

The judge in the prison still had his job to do, and there came a day when he showed me papers that could mean not only my death sentence but also the death sentence of family and friends.

"Can you explain these papers?" he asked.

"No, I can't," I admitted.

Suddenly he took all the papers and threw them into the stove! When I saw the flames destroy those condemning papers, I knew I had been guarded by divine power and understood as never before Colossians 2:14:

> Blotting out the handwriting of ordinances that was against us, which was contrary to us, (Jesus) took it out of the way, nailing it to his cross.
>
> KJV

Lord, we thank You for Your constant protection for Your ocean of love and forgiveness.

January 23

Jesus has taken all of the evidence against us and has nailed it to the cross for you and me. There are many dangerous papers in our lives, and we all must come before God on Judgment Day. Have we refused Jesus in this life? Then we will be lost. Have we received Jesus in this life? Then we have nothing to fear, for He destroyed the papers that were against us when He died on the cross for you and me. What a joy!

> At the Cross, at the Cross,
> Where I first saw the light,
> And the burden of my heart rolled away,
> It was there by faith I received my sight. . . .
>
> Ralph E. Hudson

I, I am the Lord, and besides me there is no savior.
Isaiah 43:11 RSV

Thank You, Jesus, for taking our sins upon Yourself, that we might be saved.

January 24

In our World War II prison camp, Betsie and I had to go on roll call very early in the bitterly cold morning. Sometimes we would be sent too early. Then we would take a chance and walk quietly around the camp. Everything was black. There was no light anywhere.

In that cold blackness, Betsie and I walked with the Lord and talked with the Lord. Betsie said something, I said something, then the Lord said something. How? I don't know, but we both understood what He said. That was a little bit of heaven in the midst of hell.

Lo, I am with you always, to the end of the world.
Matthew 28:20 KJV

Lord, help me to speak with You always, especially in my times of darkness, and to listen when You speak to me.

January 25

Once, while we were on roll call, a cruel guard kept us standing for a long, long time. Suddenly a skylark began to sing in the sky, and all the prisoners looked up to listen to that bird's song. As I looked at the bird I saw the sky, and I thought of Psalms 103:11. O love of God, how deep and great; far deeper than man's deepest hate. God sent that skylark daily for three weeks, exactly during roll call, to turn our eyes away from the cruelty of men to the ocean of His love.

> For as the heaven is high above the earth, so great is his mercy toward them that fear him.
> Psalms 103:11 KJV

Thank You, Lord, that You are always willing to turn our eyes in the right direction unto You.

January 26

Surrender to the Lord is not a tremendous sacrifice, not an agonizing performance. It is the most sensible thing you can do.

> Who trusts in God's unchanging love
> Builds on the rock that naught can move.
> George Neumark
> Tr. by Catherine Winkeworth

> Trust in the Lord for ever, for the Lord God is an everlasting rock.
> Isaiah 26:4 RSV

Who can direct our lives better than You, O Lord? Whom else should we trust? Certainly not ourselves!

January 27

It is dangerous to live as a halfway Christian in this age filled with darkness, chaos, and hopelessness. In the center of a hurricane there is absolute quiet and peace. There is no safer place than in the center of the will of God.

> I know your works: you are neither cold nor hot.
> . . . Therefore I counsel you to buy from me gold
> refined by fire, that you may be rich. . . .
> Revelation 3:15, 18 RSV

Lord, I know that when You ask us a question there are only two answers, yes or no (or nothing, which is the same as no). Show me what my answer meant.

January 28

What can hinder our surrender? Sins, sorrows, possessions, family, our will, rights and duties. Sins such as doubt, fear, inferiority feelings, materialism, envy, self-centeredness and self-consciousness. All are the territory of the enemy.

> Search me, O God, and know my heart!
> Try me and know my thoughts!
> And see if there be any wicked way in me,
> and lead me in the way everlasting!
> Psalms 139:23, 24 RSV

Lord Jesus, put Your searchlight on my life, and show me where I need Your cleansing blood.

January 29

Do you want to receive the gift of eternal life? Jesus will make you an heir of eternal wealth, if you will receive it.

> For the wages of sin is death; but the gift of God is eternal life through Jesus Christ our Lord.
>
> Romans 6:23 KJV

O Lord, thank You that I may enjoy eternal life now, and that the best is yet to be.

January 30

A boy wrote: "Stewardship means that life is a great ship, loaded with a rich cargo to be delivered to many peoples in many places. God is the owner, but I am the captain."

> We give Thee but Thine own, Whate'er the gift may be;
> All that we have is Thine alone, A trust, O Lord, from Thee.
>
> William How

> Thanks be to God for his inexpressible gift!
>
> 2 Corinthians 9:15 RSV

Father, as a ship's owner trusts his captain to deliver the cargo safely to its destination, so do You trust us with Your blessings. Make us good captains by filling our hearts with Your Holy Spirit.

January 31

How do you think of yourself—as owner or as captain of what you possess? Are you delivering the goods? The world does not read the Bible—it reads you and me. The godly man is the ungodly man's Bible. Are you growing like Peter? Are you glowing like Stephen? Are you going like Paul?

> People will ask: "Why was I not told
> Back at the crossroads of this Jesus?"

How are they to believe in him of whom they have never heard? And how are they to hear without a preacher?

Romans 10:14 RSV

Thank You, Lord, that You will strengthen us by a dying Saviour's love, a risen Saviour's power, an ascended Saviour's prayer, and an eternal Saviour's glory.

FEBRUARY

February 1

When Jesus comes back to make a new earth, the material will be ready. The first world was also made from chaos.

> ... the earth shall be full of the knowledge of the Lord as the waters cover the sea.
>
> Isaiah 11:9 RSV

Lord Jesus, thank You that the Bible gives us the encouragement to wait for a new heaven and a new earth in which righteousness dwells.

February 2

In describing the Jews, God called them the people whom He had formed for Himself, that they might declare His praise (*see* Isaiah 43:21). Israel is setting the stage for the last act of the history of this world. God said to Abraham, "I will bless those who bless you . . ." (Genesis 12:3 RSV).

> Through many people long since gone
> God's gracious providence has shone.
> Only one race has brought to birth
> A Sovereign fit to rule the earth;
> Its name is Israel. Oh, Jew,
> I bend my Gentile head to you.
>
> Author Unknown

I pray for the peace of Jerusalem, Lord.

February 3

Today you can read all the signs of the times, not only in the Bible but also in the newspapers. Our generation will live when these things happen, when the Lord comes. He is coming very soon!

> But you are not in darkness, brethren, for that day to surprise you like a thief.
>
> 1 Thessalonians 5:4 RSV

Thank You, Holy Spirit, that You are with us, that You give us the wisdom and vision to see the secret of God's plan and the reality of the signs of the times, but that You also give us all we need to be ready, by Your gifts and fruit.

February 4

Do nothing that you would not like to be doing when Jesus comes. Go no place where you would not like to be found when He returns.

> You must learn to know God better and discover what he wants you to do. Next, learn to put aside your own desires so that you will become patient and godly, gladly letting God have his way with you.
>
> 2 Peter 1:5, 6 LB

Lord, make me and keep me worthy to meet you at any time. Glorify Your name in my life.

February 5

Do not let the worries and cares of this life blind you so that you are unprepared for Jesus' Second Coming.

> As were the days of Noah, so will be the coming of the Son of man. For as in those days before the

flood they were eating and drinking, marrying and giving in marriage, until the day when Noah entered the ark, and they did not know until the flood came and swept them all away, so will be the coming of the Son of man.

Matthew 24:37-39 RSV

Lord Jesus, make us good soldiers in Your army, willing to experience what Paul wrote to Timothy in 2 Timothy 3:1, that in the last days it is going to be very difficult to be a Christian.

February 6

I believe that you who read this book can be ready for Jesus' coming. Why? Because all that had to be done was done at the cross!

> May the God of peace himself · sanctify you wholly; and may your spirit and soul and body be kept sound and blameless at the coming of our Lord Jesus Christ.
>
> 1 Thessalonians 5:23 RSV

We thank You for Your great sacrifice on the cross, Lord Jesus, which makes it possible for us to join You in Your final victory.

February 7

Which generation did the Lord Jesus mean when He used that word in Luke 21? The generation that is here when the signs that He foretold appear. It is our generation!

> This generation will not pass away till all has taken place.
>
> Luke 21:32 RSV

We look forward to Your coming, Lord, although we know we will have hard times before we see You.

February 8

Our knowledge of the world's future should not depress us or cause us to fear.

So when all these things begin to happen, stand straight and look up! For your salvation is near.
Luke 21:28 LB

Thank You, Lord, that Ephesians 1 reveals to us that You have allowed us to know the secret of Your plan, that You purpose in Your sovereign will that all human history shall be consummated in Christ, and that everything that exists in heaven or earth shall find its perfection and fulfillment in You.

February 9

What joy that the Bible tells us the great comfort that the best is yet to be. Our outlook goes beyond this world. We will meet the Lord in the air.

Jesus is coming for me.
What joy that will be—
His face I shall see.

We who are alive, who are left, shall be caught up together with them in the clouds to meet the Lord in the air; and so we shall always be with the Lord.
1 Thessalonians 4:17 RSV

How we long for the moment when we will be translated and see You face to face, Lord Jesus. Come quickly!

February 10

A black pastor once told me: "I do not like to read a book in which sad things happen. When I must read it, I turn to the last page. When I see that they lived happily ever after, then I can read the whole book because it has a good ending."

We must read the Bible in the same way. We tremble when we see what is going to happen before Jesus returns, but if you are afraid, read the last page. There you will see that Jesus has promised to come, and we will see Him face to face.

> Behold, I make all things new.
> > Revelation 21:5 RSV

Lord, thank You that You have told us so much about the future that we know the best is yet to be.

February 11

History is His Story. God has a schedule for your life and mine, and a schedule for the whole world. We do not know the future but we know Him who has the future in His hand. Christian, stand firm knowing that we are co-workers with God who fulfills His prophecies. Our outlook goes beyond this world to the hopeful expectation of the coming of Jesus, the Messiah, who will make all things new. In the difficult time that we are in now and which will become more difficult, a Christian is able to understand and will possess a heavenly peace that surpasses all understanding.

> (Pray) that you may be strong enough to come safely through all that is going to happen. . . .
> > Luke 21:36 Phillips

Lord Jesus, thank You that we may always look to You and expect that You will constantly care for us, and anticipate a most joyful future when Your liberation will be fulfilled.

February 12

The Second Coming of Christ will mean the end of Satan's domination in the world! The earth will be covered with the knowledge of God the way the waters cover the bottom of the sea.

> He will keep you steadfast in the faith to the end, so that when His Day comes you need fear no condemnation.
>
> 1 Corinthians 1:8 Phillips

We wait for Your victory, Lord. What a joy to know the outcome in advance!

February 13

A bishop from China told me: "I was a bishop in China for seventeen years, but I made mistakes. I did not train the lay people as evangelists. Now there are no bishops or clergy in all of China. God made lay people to be evangelists, and we had the opportunity to train them, but we did not."

Use the time you still have left to tell all the Christians you can reach that they are called to be ambassadors for Christ. They have the joyful and important calling of sharing the Good News.

> Work, for the night is coming,
> Under the sunset skies;
> While their bright tints are glowing,
> Work for daylight flies.
> Work till the last beam fadeth,
> Fadeth to shine no more;
> Work while the night is darkening,
> When man's work is o'er.
>
> Anna Coghill

(Jesus said) Go ye into all the world, and preach
the gospel to every creature.

Mark 16:15 KJV

Part of our work can be to train others, Lord. Help
us not to waste any opportunities, because circumstances can change so rapidly.

February 14

What has Jesus, the Son of God, done for us?
He left heaven and came down to earth. He humbled
Himself to be born as a baby and to be laid in a
manger. He endured the life of this world for thirty-
three years and died on a cross to bear the punish-
ment of our sin. What is He now doing in glory?
He is praying for us; He is pleading for us.

Was the only decision you made the one when
you accepted Him as your Saviour? That was important. You were born again, but you were a baby.
Is there not much more that the Lord asks from
you now?

I appeal to you therefore, brethren, by the mercies
of God, to present your bodies as a living sacrifice,
holy and acceptable to God, which is your spiritual
worship.

Romans 12:1 RSV

Lord Jesus, what a lot You did for me. When I
look at what I have done for You, I realize that
I may, I must, surrender my all to You today. Love
others through me, Lord.

February 15

We are Christ's ambassadors. An ambassador
is sent forth in an official capacity by a nation's
government to represent that government in the territory of another nation. His authority is not

measured by his own personal abilities, but is in direct proportion to the authority of the government he represents.

> You did not choose me, but I chose you and appointed you that you should go and bear fruit and that your fruit should abide. . . .
>
> John 15:16 RSV

Father, I am happy to serve as Your ambassador, secure in the authority that supports me. Thank You that I stand in Your ability.

February 16

Many nations are toppling, and we are linked so closely to them that we could also fall if we do not turn in great throngs to God, imploring Him for mercy in this immediate and alarming crisis.

> Show us Your mercy, O Lord, and grant us Your salvation.
>
> See Psalms 85:7 KJV

Father, give us strength to bring Your Word to vast numbers of people. We need more soldiers who believe that Jesus is Victor.

February 17

In the work of evangelism we are sent by the same Person, we are sent by the same power, we are sent to the same place, we are sent for the same purpose, as Jesus was. I am glad that here in America and in many other countries there is so much good training material. I mention two organizations, Campus Crusade for Christ and the Navigators, whose material we may always use to help and train others.

I have given you an example, that you also should
do as I have done to you.

> John 13:15 RSV

Lord, open our eyes so that we recognize every opportunity to bring the Gospel. Thank You that by Your indwelling in us, You make us mirrors of Your love.

February 18

When you bring God's Word to others, you must maintain the horizontal and the vertical connection with both them and the Holy Spirit. Pray in your heart for the guidance, insight, and wisdom you need.

> I will give you a mouth and wisdom, which none of
> your adversaries will be able to withstand or contradict.

> Luke 21:15 RSV

Lord, thank You for Your presence while we work. By ourselves we are too weak, but Your Spirit makes us able.

February 19

To be used to save souls for eternity is worth suffering and dying. The salvation of the lost should concern us more than our own earthly existence.

> By this we know love, that he laid down his life
> for us; and we ought to lay down our lives for the
> brethren.

> 1 John 3:16 RSV

Lord Jesus, please give us Your love and concern for those who are lost.

February 20

There is nothing anybody else can do that can stop God from using us; the fault always lies in ourselves. We can turn everything into a testimony. Even opposition can become an open door.

> So if you are offering your gift at the altar, and there remember that your brother has something against you, leave your gift there before the altar and go; first be reconciled to your brother, and then come and offer your gift.
>
> Matthew 5:23, 24 RSV

Father, when we are free of sin, we can do Your work. When we seem to be ineffective in Your work, move us to reexamine our lives for sin.

February 21

When a house is on fire and you know that there are people in it, it is a sin to straighten pictures in that house. When the world about you is in great danger, works that are in themselves not sinful can be quite wrong.

> Look carefully then how you walk, not as unwise men but as wise, making the most of the time, because the days are evil.
>
> Ephesians 5:15, 16 RSV

Lord, open our eyes to the world around us. Use us to warn people and tell them that when we walk hand in hand with You we are safe, even in the midst of a storm, and that there is an eternity to lose or gain.

February 22

When you have heard the Gospel, you have heard the greatest story ever told about the greatest offer ever made, by the greatest Person who ever lived! Do you want to receive this gift of eternal life for which Jesus left heaven and died on the cross?

It was unspeakable love that thought it.
It was unspeakable life that bought it.
It was unspeakable death that wrought it.
There is unspeakable joy where He brought it.

In this was manifested the love of God toward us. . . .
1 John 4:9 KJV

Holy Spirit, help me to understand a little more of these wonderful riches.

February 23

Jesus loves you so much that if you were the only person on earth, He would still have been willing to die for you on the cross.

I've found a Friend, O such a Friend!
He bled, He died to save me;
And not alone the gift of life
But His own self He gave me. . . .
James G. Small

. . . we have been sanctified through the body of Jesus Christ.
See Hebrews 10:10 RSV

Lord Jesus, such love is beyond our understanding. We can only say, "Thank You."

February 24

"How can I become a child of God?"
Make a clear-cut decision and say, "Yes, Lord Jesus, come into my heart."
"Is it as simple as that?"

It is. Salvation is a gift. You need only accept it and you belong to God, and He to you.

All that had to be done was finished by Jesus on the cross.

> Behold, I stand at the door, and knock: if any man hear my voice, and open the door, I will come in to him. . . .
>
> Revelation 3:20 KJV

Thank You, Lord, that I may open the door of my heart. What a joy that You come in!

February 25

"Does going to church regularly make one a Christian?"

No, you find there the nourishment you need and the fellowship with other Christians, but it is not where you are that is important but what happens in your heart. A mouse born in a biscuit tin is not a biscuit, and a dog who lives in a garage is no automobile.

> If you confess with your lips that Jesus is Lord and believe in your heart that God raised him from the dead, you will be saved.
>
> Romans 10:9 RSV

Lord, thank You that I am a Christian because *You* died on the cross almost two thousand years ago and You could say, "It is finished." All that needed to be done was done by You. Thank You, thank You, Lord Jesus.

February 26

Conversion is not a blind leap into the darkness. It is a joyous leap into the light that is the love of God.

I am the light of the world; he who follows me will
not walk in darkness, but will have the light of life.

John 8:12 RSV

The human side in us fears the unknown, Lord. Give
us the faith we need to step out of our dim caves
and into Your guiding light.

February 27

"What happens after I say yes to the Lord?"
Then you may claim all of God's promises in
the Bible. Your sins, your worries, your life—you
may cast them all on Him.

I am come that they might have life, and that they
might have it more abundantly.

John 10:10 KJV

Lord, forgive us that too often we live as beggars
when we are children of the King of Kings and im-
measurably rich.

February 28

"When I have accepted Jesus as my Saviour,
what must I do to grow?"
Be filled with the Holy Spirit, join a church where
the members believe the Bible and know the Lord,
seek the fellowship of other Christians, learn and
be nourished by God's Word and His many promises.
Conversion is not the end of your journey—it is only
the beginning.

Thy word is a lamp to my feet and a light to my
path.

Psalms 119:105 RSV

Lord, thank You that You have provided our spiritual
nourishment through Your Spirit, Your Word, the
Bible, and through the fellowship of the saints.

February 29

I am eighty-five years old and I am so thankful that I am able to continue the work I love. God has a plan for every life. All of us are called to be the light of the world wherever He places us. We are within His perfect guidance when we trust and obey Him. A tool does not decide where to work. It is the Master who decides where it is to be used.

> For we are his workmanship, created in Christ Jesus for good works, which God prepared beforehand, that we should walk in them.
>
> Ephesians 2:10 RSV

Lord, we may look forward to retirement from our earthly work, but You will use us wherever You guide us. What a privilege!

MARCH

March 1

So many people are like tightrope walkers. In one hand they have a sack filled with their unjust past, in the other hand a sack filled with the anticipated future. They are balancing between hope and despair. That attitude is wrong.

Have you the Holy Spirit, or has the Holy Spirit you?

> God has not given us a spirit of fear, but a spirit of power and love and a sound mind.
>
> 2 Timothy 1:7 Phillips

Lord, with our weak hand in Your strong hand, we walk so victoriously.

March 2

Is Jesus your guest only in a little attic room? Then nobody knows He is there. His strength to protect you in the other rooms is lost. Throw open all the doors!

> You shall love the Lord your God with all your heart, and with all your soul, and with all your mind.
>
> Matthew 22:37 RSV

O Lord Jesus, fill my house, my heart, my life with Your presence.

March 3

Our fight is not against any physical enemy; it is against organizations and powers that are spiritual. We must struggle against sin all our lives, but we are assured we will win. We stand on the front line of the battle. A compromise can be dangerous.

We are up against the unseen power that controls this dark world, and spiritual agents from the very headquarters of evil.

Ephesians 6:12 Phillips

Lord, thank You that even when we have fought to a standstill, we may still stand our ground.

March 4

Perfect obedience would be perfect happiness, if only we had perfect confidence in the power we were obeying. A wolf does not bother a sheep that is with the flock, close to the shepherd.

The Lord is my shepherd; I shall not want.

Psalm 23:1 RSV

Keep me in Your flock, Lord, safe and secure in Your protection, knowing I have nothing to fear when I do Your work.

March 5

When the Lord takes your sins, you never see them again. He casts them into the depths of the sea, forgiven and forgotten. I even believe that He places a sign over them that reads *no fishing allowed.*

As far as the east is from the west, so far does he remove our transgressions from us.

Psalms 103:12 RSV

Lord, we know this because the Bible tells us so. Keep our eyes in the right direction, unto You, by Your Holy Spirit.

March 6

Are you experiencing prayer problems? The Holy Spirit will help you. When we are totally inadequate, the Spirit is interceding with God the Father for us.

> . . . for we do not know how to pray as we ought, but the Spirit himself intercedes for us with sighs too deep for words.
>
> Romans 8:26 RSV

O Holy Spirit, what a joy that we may bring our prayer problems to You. You see us, You see the enemy, You see the world around us, and You bring God's love instead of our confusion into our hearts. Hallelujah!

March 7

"May I pray about the little problems of my life, or only about the big ones?"

One day when I had a bad cold in the concentration camp, Betsie, my sister, prayed for a handkerchief for me. We laughed at the silliness of that prayer, but only a few minutes later a woman came by with a handkerchief for me! We do not know what God considers important. We do know that He answers prayers—even tiny ones.

> You do not have, because you do not ask.
>
> James 4:2 RSV

Father, You care, and will not be angered when we ask for very small things, for we are Your children.

March 8

A little girl cried because her very old doll was broken. Her father said, "Bring me your doll." Then he repaired it. Why did that grown-up man give his time to mend such a worthless, ugly doll? He saw the doll through the eyes of the little one, because he loved his little daughter. So God sees your problems through your eyes because He loves you.

> For as the heavens are high above the earth, so great is his steadfast love toward those who fear him.
>
> Psalms 103:11 RSV

Father, what a joy it is to know that we are Your children and live within Your constant care.

March 9

"It is so hard to pray!"

Yes, even the disciples had to ask the Lord how to pray. If you cannot pray, confess it to the Lord and He will make you able.

> ... one of his disciples said to him, "Lord, teach us to pray, as John taught his disciples."
>
> Luke 11:1 RSV

Lord, we realize that when we pray we are at a place of strategic importance. The devil laughs when we are up to our ears in work, but he trembles when we pray. Guide and protect us and bless our prayer life.

March 10

"I am so busy. How can I find time to pray?"
Ask for forgiveness. Ask to be cleansed of the

sin of having no time to pray. We must begin and end the day with prayer. It could be that Satan is pushing you into too much work so that you cannot take time to pray.

> But we will devote ourselves to prayer and to the ministry of the word.
>> Acts 6:4 RSV

Lord, forgive us that we too often major in minors. Thank You that we *may* pray.

March 11

"Does God always give us what we ask in prayer?"

Sometimes His answer is no. He knows what we do not know. He knows everything and His negative answer is part of His plan for our lives.

> My life is but a weaving, between my God
>> and me.
> I do not choose the colors, He worketh
>> steadily.
> Ofttimes He weaveth sorrow, and I in foolish
>> pride,
> Forget He sees the upper, and I the underside.
>
> Not till the loom is silent and the shuttles
>> cease to fly,
> Will God unroll the canvas and explain the
>> reason why.
> The dark threads are as needful in the skillful
>> Weaver's hand,
> As the threads of gold and silver in the pattern
>> He has planned.

> I know, O Lord, that thy judgments are right, and that in faithfulness thou hast afflicted me.
>> Psalms 119:75 RSV

Lord, it is hard to accept a negative answer, but keep us humble enough, patient enough, faithful enough to trust. Thank You that You always answer our prayers in Your way with a yes or a no. How good it is to know that You never make a mistake.

March 12

"It is all so simple!"

Yes, the truth is simple, but very deep. The complications come from ourselves or the devil.

Jesus did it; the Bible tells it.

I believe it; that settles it.

In the beginning was the Word. . . .
                                              John 1:1 KJV

Thank You, Lord, that even a child can understand it.

March 13

Are you bothered by temptations? Temptation is not a sin. Even Jesus was tempted. The Lord Jesus gives you the strength needed to resist temptation. A tempted child of God is still a child of God. Confess your sins, claim the victory of Jesus as your own, and defeat temptation.

For because he himself has suffered and been tempted, he is able to help those who are tempted.
                                    Hebrews 2:18 RSV

Lord, thank You that when we face temptation You always give us a way to escape.

March 14

Guilt is a useful experience because it shows where things are wrong. It is dangerous when it is not there at all, just as the absence of pain when someone is ill can be dangerous.

When we belong to Jesus we are not called to carry our guilt ourselves. God has laid on Jesus the sins of the whole world. What you have to do is to tell Him everything, confess your guilt and sin and repent, and then He will cleanse you and throw all your sins into the depths of the sea. Don't forget there is a sign that reads *no fishing allowed.* If somebody has suffered through your guilt, then make restitution in the power and wisdom of the Lord.

> As far as the east is from the west, so far does he remove our transgressions from us.
>
> Psalms 103:12 RSV

Lord, thank You that where You have carried our guilt we have not to carry it ourselves. Help us not to listen to the accuser of the brethren, the devil, anymore, but to Your Holy Spirit, who always points to the finished work on the cross.

March 15

The blood of Jesus does not cleanse excuses. It cleanses sins that are confessed. We have to humble ourselves.

> ... the blood of Jesus his Son cleanses us from all sin. If we say we have no sin, we deceive ourselves, and the truth is not in us.
>
> 1 John 1:7, 8 RSV

Father, help us, through Your Holy Spirit, to keep the eyes of our understanding clear, so that we see our sins as severely as they should be seen, but also that we see the ocean of Your love and grace.

March 16

What a respectable sin self-pity is! It can be so logical, convincing you that you are suffering terribly. It brings darkness, despair, even illness.

> ... I have learned to be content, whatever the circumstances may be. I know now how to live when things are difficult and I know how to live when things are prosperous. In general and in particular I have learned the secret of facing either poverty or plenty. I am ready for anything through the strength of the One Who lives within me.
>
> Philippians 4:11-13 Phillips

Lord, help us to keep our minds on You. Then we accept both poverty and plenty in Your strength.

March 17

There is only One who can cleanse us from our sins—He who made us.

In Russia, many people lived in a certain apartment house. The basement of the house was filled with the junk of all the families. Amongst the junk was a beautiful harp, which nobody had been able to fix.

One snowy night, a tramp asked if he could sleep in the building. The people cleared a space for him in the corner of the basement, and he was happy to stay there.

In a little while, the people heard beautiful music coming from the basement. The owner of the harp rushed downstairs and found the tramp playing it.

"But how could you repair it? We couldn't," he said.

The tramp smiled and replied, "I made this harp years ago, and when you make something, you can also repair it."

All things were made by him; and without him
was not any thing made that was made.

John 1:3 KJV

Lord, You made me. What joy that You are willing
and able to repair me.

March 18

Jesus said, "Occupy till I come." Do you think
you have no opportunity to do this? I met a woman
in Russia who had multiple sclerosis. Her feet and
hands were paralyzed except for one finger. With
that one finger she typed out Bible texts and in-
spirational books.

> Put up with your share of hardship as a loyal
> soldier in Christ's army.

2 Timothy 2:3 Phillips

What joy that You can use me even when I am weak.

March 19

This paralyzed woman's husband bound her
typewritten messages together into books which
then went from one person to another. She did this
work until the day she died. She is now with the
Lord. How happy she is! And I am sure that she
has heard from many there who have read her
literature, "It was you who invited me here." Do
not say you are not healthy or strong enough—you
have more than one finger to use for God's work!

> Never lose your sense of urgency, in season or out
> of season. Prove, correct, and encourage, using the
> utmost patience in your teaching.

2 Timothy 4:2 Phillips

Lord, we claim Your strength to serve You, no
matter what our circumstances are.

March 20

If we follow Jesus in all things, many times we will be misunderstood. Bitterness may creep into our hearts. But it is not our job to convince our friends. All we must do is deal with our own sins.

Search me, O God, and know my heart!
Try me and know my thoughts!
And see if there be any wicked way in me,
and lead me in the way everlasting!
Psalms 139:23, 24 RSV

When people cause me to feel anger, or to feel wronged, cleanse me from the sins of my emotions, Lord Jesus. Show me where *I* need Your forgiveness.

March 21

Forgiveness is the key which unlocks the door of resentment and the handcuffs of hatred. It breaks the chains of bitterness and the shackles of selfishness. The forgiveness of Jesus not only takes away our sins but it also makes them as if they had never been. That is the way we must forgive. The Holy Spirit makes us able to do it through the love of God which He brings into our hearts.

. . . forgive, and you will be forgiven.
Luke 6:37 RSV

Lord, help me to forgive in Your way.

March 22

Avoid gossip and slander. We shall all be judged one day by the standards of Jesus, not man. We have to answer only to God for our actions.

Remember, as you point one finger at another person, three fingers of your hand point back at you.

Why, then, criticise your brother's actions, why try to make him look small? We shall all be judged one day, not by each other's standards or even our own, but by the standard of Christ.

Romans 14:10 Phillips

After all, who are you to criticise the servant of somebody else, especially when that Somebody Else is God? It is to his own Master that he gives, or fails to give, satisfactory service. And don't doubt that satisfaction, for God is well able to transform men into servants who are satisfactory.

Romans 14:4 Phillips

Father, forgive me my criticism.

March 23

When we forgive someone, we must not be surprised when old, angry thoughts return to us. The same is true for our confessed sins. We may be tempted, or even fall back, but we have been delivered from our sins, and the temptation will gradually fade from our lives.

No temptation has overtaken you that is not common to man. God is faithful, and he will not let you be tempted beyond your strength, but with the temptation will also provide the way of escape, that you may be able to endure it.

1 Corinthians 10:13 RSV

Holy Spirit, teach us how to receive forgiveness, to forgive others, and to forgive ourselves.

March 24

Two men died on the same day, one on a hill, one in a valley. He who died on the hill prayed for the men who killed Him, and during His terrible suffering He had compassion for His mother. His name was Jesus. The other man killed himself on the tree that he had chosen. His name was Judas. When you make room for Jesus in your heart, He will give you His love in life and in death.

> There are three things that remain—faith, hope, and love—and the greatest of these is love.
>
> 1 Corinthians 13:13 LB

Lord Jesus, thank You that in life and in death I belong to You. Hallelujah!

March 25

God placed all our sins on Jesus. Jesus paid the penalty for our sins, purchasing a place for us in heaven. Faith in Him is the key that opens the door to heaven.

> For by grace you have been saved through faith; and this is not your own doing, it is the gift of God —not because of works, lest any man should boast.
>
> Ephesians 2:8, 9 RSV

Thank You, Jesus, that we may look unto You, the author and finisher of our faith. Will You make it grow with every passing day?

March 26

The precious blessing of Easter is that we have a living Saviour! The Lord is risen. He is risen indeed!

> And he said to them, "Do not be amazed; you seek Jesus of Nazareth, who was crucified. He has risen, he is not here; see the place where they laid him."
>
> Mark 16:6 RSV

We yearn to keep the precious blessing of Easter in our hearts throughout the year, Lord Jesus. Will You, through Your Holy Spirit, fill our hearts with the knowledge and surety that You live.

March 27

We must not be too dependent on meetings. You and I are what we are when we are alone. Find your satisfaction in Jesus Christ. Talk with Him, listen to Him, look at Him.

I can do all things through Christ which strengtheneth me.

Philippians 4:13 KJV

Lord, make me independent of conditions. I thank You that You are the same yesterday, today, and forever.

March 28

Feelings come and feelings go
And feelings are deceiving.
My warrant is the Word of God,
None else is worth believing.

But the word of the Lord abides for ever. That word is the good news which was preached to you.

1 Peter 1:25 RSV

Lord, help us to rule our feelings and to control them so that they do not control us. We take our orders from Your Word and the Holy Spirit, not from our emotions.

March 29

The Bible is a weapon. It can be used for offense and defense. When you meet Satan with authority, the authority of the Word, he will depart.

> O Word of God Incarnate,
> O Wisdom from on high,
> O Truth unchanged, unchanging,
> O Light of our dark sky:
> We praise Thee for the radiance
> That from the hallowed page,
> A lantern to our footsteps,
> Shines on from age to age.
>
> William How

He sendeth out his word. . . .

Psalms 147:18 KJV

Lord, We thank You for the weapon that is Your Word. It contains all we need to know to be victorious.

March 30

Sometimes in my watchmaker's shop I would be asked to repair a brand-new watch which did not keep time properly. Instead of trying to fix it, I would send it back to the manufacturer.

That is what we must do with our faith. If something is wrong with your faith, send it back to Jesus for repair. He can fix it perfectly.

> . . . let us run with patience the race that is set before us, Looking unto Jesus the author and finisher of our faith. . . .
>
> Hebrews 12:1, 2 KJV

Lord Jesus, as You gave us our faith, so You can make it whole. Lead us back to You when we need completion.

March 31

Prayer is such an important power. In the concentration camp, seven hundred of us lived in a room built for two hundred people. We were all dirty, nervous, and tense. One day a horrible fight broke out amongst the prisoners. Betsie began to pray aloud. It was as if a storm laid down, until at last all was quiet. Then Betsie said, "Thank You, Father." A tired old woman was used by the Lord to save the situation for seven hundred fellow prisoners through her prayers.

> Here then is my charge. First, supplications, prayers, intercessions and thanksgivings should be made on behalf of all men. . . ."
>
> 1 Timothy 2:1 Phillips

There may be days of darkness and distress,
When sin has power to tempt, and care to press.
Yet in the darkest day I will not fear,
For 'midst the shadows, You will still be near.
Thank You, Lord Jesus.

APRIL

April 1

Could a mariner sit idle
When he heard the drowning cry?
Could a doctor sit in comfort
Knowing that his patients die?
Could a fireman watch men perish
And not give a helping hand?
Can you sit at ease in Sion
With a world around condemned?

For whoever is ashamed of me and of my words, of
him will the Son of man be ashamed when he comes
in his glory and the glory of the Father and of the
holy angels.

Luke 9:26 RSV

O Lord, forgive me that I have been blind to the
urgency of bringing the Gospel.

April 2

We can only understand God's purpose for this
world, and what it is to be His ambassadors, when
we are born again. Then we truly know Jesus. It
is exciting to be in God's school! As His personal
representatives we may say, "Make your peace with
God."

Unless one is born anew, he cannot see the kingdom of God.

John 3:3 RSV

Lord Jesus, show me if I am Your child, born into Your family. What a joy to know that if there is any doubt, I may open my heart for You to come in, and I am sure that you will perform that miracle by which I will become a child of God.

April 3

There is no army where only officers fight. Everyone who is in the army of God must fight, even the soldier in the lowest rank. When we obey and act on the promises, we stand on victory ground, because the ability of our Master is available to us.

As the Father has sent me, even so I send you.
John 20:21 RSV

God give us men touched with fire from above.
God give us men with a Calvary love.
God give us men who are filled with Your power.
God give us men for this day and this hour.
Men who are fearless when seeking the lost,
Men who will follow whatever the cost.
Where are the men we need?
Where are the men?
When will they heed thy call,
When, Saviour, when?
Raise up a host burning with holy fire,
Men filled with Thee and with flaming desire.
Men who will serve Thee without doubt, without fear.
God give us men who will now volunteer.

Lesley Dewell

April 4

An East German teacher was telling her class that God does not exist. After her lesson, she asked who still believed in God, and a little girl stood up. The teacher made her stay after school and write one hundred times, "I do not believe that God exists." The girl could not do that, so she wrote, "I *do* believe that God exists." The teacher was so angry with her that she made her write it correctly one thousand times at home that night. The little girl wrote it one thousand times *her* way, although she knew she would be punished severely in school the next day.

> Blessed are those who are persecuted for righteousness' sake, for theirs is the kingdom of heaven.
> Matthew 5:10 RSV

Lord, though we suffer for our faith, we will persevere with Your help. Your strength will be demonstrated even in our weakness. Hallelujah!

April 5

To travel through the desert with others, to suffer thirst, to find a spring, to drink of it, and not to tell the others, that they may be spared, is exactly the same as enjoying Christ and not telling others about Him.

> As every man hath received the gift, even so minister the same one to another, as good stewards of the manifold grace of God.
> 1 Peter 4:10 KJV

Lord, I must humble myself. I have been selfish.

April 6

The wisdom of men, even the voice of our own senses, should not be used to try to understand the Bible. Don't worry about what you do not understand of the Bible. Worry about what you do understand and do not live by.

> By faith we understand that the world was created by the word of God, so that what is seen was made out of things which do not appear.
>
> Hebrews 11:3 RSV

Father, let us know when to be satisfied with not knowing. We do not need great wisdom to trust in You.

April 7

Only faith will make us see the reality of Christ's victory. Our senses are sometimes limited by our intellect; faith has no limitations and sees the truth.

> Now faith is the substance of things hoped for, the evidence of things not seen.
>
> Hebrews 11:1 KJV

Thank You, Lord, that Your foolishness is the greatest wisdom. All is ours through faith. Help us to accept the great gifts offered to us. We will take and enjoy them, and not wonder about the wrappings they come in.

April 8

Self is a tight lock. I see many decent sinners who are in a spiritual prison because their self is on the throne of their hearts and Jesus is on the cross. What liberation comes when Jesus cleanses their hearts with His blood and comes to the throne, and self goes on the cross!

> He who finds his life will lose it, and he who loses his life for my sake will find it.
>
> Matthew 10:39 RSV

Lord Jesus, come on the throne of my heart. I am willing to give of myself, to take up my cross, and follow You.

April 9

If you make a compromise with surrender, you can remain interested in the abundant life, all the riches of freedom, love, and peace, but it is the same as looking at a display in a shop window. You look through the window but do not go in and buy. You will not pay the price—Surrender.

E. Stanley Jones

> Truly, truly, I say to you, unless a grain of wheat falls into the earth and dies, it remains alone; but if it dies, it bears much fruit.
>
> John 12:24 RSV

Lord, what joy it is to belong to You, to live in the realm of life abundant now, and to know that the best is yet to be. Hallelujah!

April 10

We are representatives from heaven to this earth. I learned from the astronauts, who were representatives from the earth to the moon, that 100 percent obedience was necessary for them. Jesus, by His obedience to the Father, taught how we can be like Him.

And being found in human form he humbled himself and became obedient unto death, even death on
a cross.

Philippians 2:8 RSV

Father, if we would lead others to You, we must
obey Your will. Show us where we have failed.

April 11

An astronaut was drilling to see if there was
something deep in the crust of the moon. The drilling was hard work, and he asked the leader on earth
if he might stop. His leader said no. The astronaut
did not argue, but worked on until he found what
he was seeking.

Isn't that a good example of what we must do?
We ask, "Lord, may I stop?" The Lord says, "No,
go on." We must trust that in obedience we will
reach the goal.

God is at work in you, both to will and to work for
his good pleasure. Do all things without grumbling
or questioning.

Philippians 2:13, 14, RSV

Lord, may our obedience shine forth to others as
a beacon, urging them on until You declare the
job complete.

April 12

Because their situation was serious and dangerous, I am sure that the astronauts did not quarrel
about little things. They saw things in the right proportion: great things great, small things small. They
had faith in their chief, in their equipment, and in
their calling.

Above all taking the shield of faith, with which you can quench all the flaming darts of the evil one.
See Ephesians 6:16 RSV

Lord, give us vision on our lives, and on the world around us, so that we may see things, as it were, from Your point of view.

April 13

So often we do not live as richly as is possible because our unwillingness to yield stands in the way. Yield! What God does not have at His disposal, He cannot sanctify. Let His will be your will, His way your way, and all insufficiency and earthly ineptitude will be met by the sufficiency of His grace.

> Make me a captive, Lord,
> And then I shall be free;
> Force me to render up my sword,
> And I shall conqueror be.
> I sink in life's alarms
> When by myself I stand;
> Imprison me within Thine arms,
> And strong shall be my hand.
>
> George Matheson

Humble yourselves therefore under the mighty hand of God. . . .
1 Peter 5:6 RSV

Lord, make me willing to be made willing to do Your will.

April 14

When you live a surrendered life, God is willing and able to provide for your every need.

... your Father knows what you need before you ask him.

Matthew 6:8 RSV

Lord, show me where I still try to provide my own needs. Teach me, by Your Holy Spirit, to trust You.

April 15

It is Jesus who restores any broken connection between God and us. I remember when my connection was broken by disobedience. I said, "Lord, I will go everywhere You send me, but never send me to Germany." When I did not receive any guidance, I asked if there was disobedience in my life. The Lord said, "Germany." The very moment I decided to obey, my connection was restored! And how God blessed my time in that country!

By faith Abraham obeyed when he was called to go out to a place which he was to receive as an inheritance. . . .

Hebrews 11:8 RSV

Lord, I do not ask to see the distant scene. One step is enough for me.

April 16

Never be afraid to trust an unknown future to a known God. God looks for men who trust Him fully; in them He will show His power.

Thou art my rock and my fortress; for thy name's sake lead me and guide me.

Psalms 31:3 RSV

Jesus, Saviour, pilot me
Over life's tempestuous sea.
Unknown waves before me roll,

Hiding rocks and treach'rous shoal.
Chart and compass come from Thee;
Jesus, Saviour, pilot me.

Edward Hopper

April 17

Do you ask, "How do you know God's voice when you hear it?"

I answer with a question: How do you know the voices of your loved ones? You know them because you listen to them often. Listen often in obedience to the still, small voice of God.

> And your ears shall hear a word behind you, saying, "This is the way, walk in it," when you turn to the right or when you turn to the left.
> Isaiah 30:21 RSV

Father, tune our ears to Your voice, so that we may always hear Your commands and comfort.

April 18

Living in a sick and dangerous world as we do, we have a responsibility. Who will overcome the world? He who believes that Jesus is the Son of God. Our responsibility is to spread God's Word everywhere we go, so that more people will be numbered in God's family.

> For whatever is born of God overcomes the world; and this is the victory that overcomes the world, our faith. Who is it that overcomes the world but he who believes that Jesus is the Son of God?
> 1 John 5:4, 5 RSV

Yes, Lord Jesus, I believe that You are the Son of God. Does that really mean that I will be used to overcome the world? What grace, what overwhelming joy!

April 19

The most important question is not how much work is being done but how much Jesus is doing through you. Look up, God's ceiling is unlimited. Learn to look on Jesus, and more and more you will find that Jesus is directing your wandering look toward the Holy Spirit.

> I know the One in Whom I have placed my confidence, and I am perfectly certain that the work He has committed to me is safe in His Hands until that Day.
>
> 2 Timothy 1:12 Phillips

Lord, take my daily life, my work, my whole being into Your hands.

April 20

A doctor in India wrote to me:

> The great reward of the blessed work here in the leprosy hospital is to see how quickly the patients change into new, happy people. In the Hindu world, leprosy patients have no value. They learn to accept that very soon. But what a change when they find out how important they are in God's eyes!

> Not one sparrow (What do they cost? Two for a penny?) can fall to the ground without your Father knowing it. And the very hairs of your head are all numbered. So don't worry! You are more valuable to him than many sparrows.
>
> Matthew 10:29-31 LB

Father, no matter what happens to us, we know we are important in Your sight. What a joy! Thank You for that safety!

April 21

> Unfathomable His wondrous love,
> Unchangeable His ways.
> Unsearchable His blessed truths,
> Unutterable His praise.

To me, though I am the very least of all the saints, this grace was given, to preach to the Gentiles the unsearchable riches of Christ.

Ephesians 3:8 RSV

Although we understand only a part of Your mysteries, Lord, we know enough to bring men to You, for You seek the lost and are willing to use us.

April 22

The will of God is either a burden that we can carry or a power that carries us.

He who finds his life will lose it, and he who loses his life for my sake will find it.

Matthew 10:39 RSV

Lord, show me Your will today. I am happy to go Your way.

April 23

Through his attitude when he lost everything, Job can teach us a practical lesson. He could say, "The Lord has given, the Lord has taken away. Blessed be the name of the Lord."

Though he slay me, yet will I trust in him.

Job 13:15 KJV

Lord, thank You that when we go hand in hand with You, our marriage, work, ministry, and children are all part of Your victorious plan for our life.

April 24

When we work in God's Kingdom, we work for and with God.

If you work *for* God, have a committee. If you work *with* God, have a prayer meeting. God performed miracles when Peter and Cornelius met.

... Peter went up on the housetop to pray....
Acts 10:9 RSV

Cornelius prayed in his house.
See Acts 10:30 KJV

Lord, what a joy and security it is that we may, that we must, pray together.

April 25

He who cannot forgive others breaks the bridge over which he must pass, for every man has the need to be forgiven.

It is often more difficult to forgive than to ask forgiveness, but it is vital to forgive. If you do not, the other person remains in bondage, open to attacks from Satan.

And whenever you stand praying, forgive, if you have anything against any one; so that your Father also who is in heaven may forgive you your trespasses.
Mark 11:25, 26 RSV

Father, remind us to forgive. We are often so busy asking for our own forgiveness that we forget others, or we deliberately withhold our forgiveness.

April 26

Hatred is like a room that is dark during the daytime. You do not need to waste energy by turn-

ing on all the lights inside. The darkness will go
when you let the sun in by opening the curtains.

Let God's love fill your heart and the darkness
of hatred will find no room.

> He who says he is in the light and hates his brother
> is in the darkness still.
>
> 1 John 2:9 RSV

Thank You, Jesus, that You have brought into our
hearts God's love through the Holy Spirit. Thank
You, Father, that Your love in us is victorious over
our unforgiving spirits, our resentment, and our
hatred.

April 27

Do you ask, "Is Jesus able?"

I can say, "Yes, and you have the victory through
Him." Don't believe what your emotions tell you.
Believe what God's Word tells you. Your emotions
must be redeemed by Jesus.

> Coward and wayward and weak,
> I change with the changing sky.
> Today so eager and brave,
> Tomorrow not willing to try.
> But He never gives in,
> And we two will win,
> Jesus and I.

> . . . the victory belongs to the Lord.
>
> Proverbs 21:31 RSV

Lord, it is sometimes hard for us to see our victories,
but we know that they are there. Thank You that
Your Word tells us so clearly that together with
You we stand on victory ground.

April 28

Peter said in 2 Peter 1:5-7: "Make every effort to supplement your faith with virtue, and virtue with knowledge, and knowledge with self-control, and self-control with steadfastness, and steadfastness with godliness, and godliness with brotherly affection, and brotherly affection with love" (RSV).

Is that too high an aim? It would be if you and I had to do it in our own strength. But praise the Lord, it is all the fruit of the Spirit.

> The fruit of the Spirit is love, joy, peace, patience, kindness, goodness, faithfulness, gentleness, self-control. . . .
>
> Galatians 5:22, 23 RSV

Thank You, Lord, that Your Holy Spirit does the job. Fill me. You and I together are more than conquerors.

April 29

I once spoke to a group of prisoners about the text "You are the light of the world." I showed them that after they received the Lord Jesus as their Saviour, they had the duty of being the light in the darkness of that prison.

One of the men said, "Fellows, this morning I read in the Bible about three murderers. One's name was Moses, one's was David, and one's was Paul. We know them as heroes of God, but all three were also murderers. Look what God did with this trio of murderers! There is hope for you, fellows—and for me."

> You are the light of the world.
>
> Matthew 5:14 RSV

Lord, thank You that You were willing to use murderers such as Moses, David, and Paul. Thank You that You want to use me, a sinner saved by grace.

April 30

We are common earthenware jars, filled with the treasure of the riches of God. The jar is not important—the treasure is everything.

> But we have this treasure in earthen vessels, that the excellency of the power may be of God, and not of us.
>
> 2 Corinthians 4:7 KJV

Father, it is a testimony to Your glory that something so common as our weak bodies may possess Your riches. Only a true Artist can make full use of humble materials.

MAY

May 1

Both the devil and the Spirit of God make us conscious of sin. The devil tells us that the sin we committed was exactly our nature and that there is no hope for us, that we have to remain that way for the rest of our lives. He is a liar. Listen to what the Holy Spirit tells us through the Bible. The glory is that the Spirit of God directs His floodlight on the cross.

> My hope is built on nothing less
> Than Jesus' blood and righteousness;
> I dare not trust the sweetest frame,
> But wholly lean on Jesus' Name.
> On Christ the solid Rock, I stand;
> All other ground is sinking sand. . . .
> Edward Mofe

And being found in human form (Christ) humbled himself and became obedient unto death. . . .
Philippians 2:8 RSV

Thank You, Holy Spirit, that You turn our eyes away from our sins and toward the cross.

May 2

Seek the Lord. Keep seeking through prayer, Bible study, and fellowship with other Christians. Give Him an opportunity to multiply what He gave you. He longs to open His resources to you. God is more grieved by powerless Christians than by powerful atheists.

> God is able to make all grace abound toward you;
> that ye, always having all sufficiency in all things,
> may abound to every good work.
>
> 2 Corinthians 9:8 KJV

Lord, we will seek You constantly so that You may increase our worth to Your work. But what joy we know we shall find, because You found us. Hallelujah!

May 3

Jesus went from victory to victory, not from defeat to victory, as we do. Jesus prayed for you and me two thousand years ago!

> I do not pray for these only, but also for those
> who believe in me through their word.
>
> John 17:20 RSV

Thank You, Lord Jesus, that You were my intercessor and that You are now also the One who intercedes for me.

May 4

The Return of the Lord to Heaven (a legend):

The angels gave Him a fantastic welcome,
And they gathered around Him, full of questions,
About His death, resurrection and ascension.
"What is it all about?" they asked.
"The redemption of the world," He replied.
"But You have come back here. How will the world know about it?"
"I have trained My men."
"To evangelize the whole world?"
"Yes, indeed, every corner of it."
"How many men did You train for such a mammoth task?"

"A handful."

"A handful? But what if they fail?"

"If they fail, I have made no other plans."

"But is that not a great risk to take?"

"No, they will not fail."

> . . . as they were looking on, (Jesus) was lifted up, and a cloud took him out of their sight.
>
> Acts 1:9 RSV

Lord Jesus, thank You for Your faith in us and our faith in You, which keeps us from failing.

May 5

Many people hesitate to accept Jesus because it would mean giving up a sin they have grown fond of. They know they are too weak. Yet, if they put their lives in Jesus' hand, He will be able to provide the needed strength! Our little sins are as deadly as our big ones. Why do we only entrust the big ones to the Lord? Surely if He was able to save our souls, He is capable of keeping us from our little sins. I will just mention a few: overeating, gossip, and self-pity.

> I take the life of victory.
> Not I, but Christ Himself in me.
> He conquers now, He sets me free.
> He gives, I take, the victory.

> . . . for when I am weak, then I am strong.
>
> 2 Corinthians 12:10 KJV

Lord, when I look at myself I must humble myself. Thank You that You know me, and that You are victorious. Keep me from becoming possessive of my sin, Lord.

May 6

The law is useful, but it does not give us the whole answer. It shows us our sins, but we need grace as the answer to our sin problem.

> Run, John, run, the law commands,
> But gives us neither feet nor hands.
> Far better news the Gospel brings,
> It bids us fly, and gives us wings.
>> John Bunyan

My grace is sufficient for thee.
See 2 Corinthians 12:9 KJV

Lord, thank You that You gave us both the law and grace.

May 7

People sometimes ask me, "Can a person be saved so quickly?" I ask them to remember Levi, the tax collector who closed his office and followed Jesus.

"But that was Jesus who asked him to come," they reply.

Yes, and who converts people now? Certainly not us! *Jesus* asks them to follow Him, and uses us, and they say yes to *Him*.

For God is at work in you, both to will and to work for his good pleasure.
Philippians 2:13 RSV

A simple yes is all we need to begin our real life when You ask, Lord. It does not matter which human teacher is used in our conversion. It is Your working through him that is important.

May 8

Study the Bible and observe how the persons behaved and how God dealt with them. There is explicit teaching on every condition of life. Often we receive an answer to our whys when we study the lives of the people in the Bible.

Read the story in Luke 8:22-25. Jesus was asleep and the lives of His disciples were in danger. They were very afraid. But Jesus awoke and there was a calm.

> He commandeth even the winds and water, and they obey him.
>
> Luke 8:25 KJV

Keep our eyes in the right direction, unto You, Lord Jesus.

May 9

There is hope for even the worst of sinners when he confesses and is cleansed by the blood of Jesus. Filled with the Holy Spirit, any man can be the light of the world. The churches do not lack great scholars and great minds. They lack men and women who can and will be channels of the power of God. They lack that which was accessible at Pentecost.

> You shall receive power when the Holy Spirit has come upon you. . . .
>
> Acts 1:8 RSV

Lord, make me a channel of blessing today.

May 10

Prayer is the same as the breathing of air for the lungs. Exhaling makes us get rid of our dirty air. Inhaling gives clean air. To exhale is to confess, to inhale is to be filled with the Holy Spirit.

I often have to confess worry. Then I just tell it to my heavenly Father. I say the word *sorry* before I say the word please.

> Have you got any rivers
> you think are uncrossable?
> Have you got any mountains
> you can't tunnel through?
> Our God specializes in things
> called impossible—
> He can do what no one else can do.

Continue steadfastly in prayer. . . .
                                        Colossians 4:2 RSV

Thank You, Holy Spirit, that You teach us how to breathe spiritually in the right way.

May 11

Some people think that I have great faith, but that is not true. I do not have great faith—I have faith in a great God! Jesus said that if we have faith no bigger than a mustard seed, it is sufficient to remove mountains. We understand that to mean that not quantity but quality is important. The joy is that the Holy Spirit is willing to bring faith into our hearts. His faith in us has power, just as a mustard seed is small but has power to bring forth fruit.

The kingdom of heaven is like a grain of mustard seed. . . .
                                        Matthew 13:31 RSV

Holy Spirit, may the faith You bring us blossom and be fruitful.

May 12

We are children of God. We are set in the midst of the most glorious campaign into which man could ever enter. We are on the noblest road that the world has ever known. This life is a preparatory school, an antechamber of heaven. Our greatest joys are but the first fruits and the foretaste of the eternal joy that is coming.

> Jesus . . . for the joy that was set before him endured the cross, despising the shame, and is seated at the right hand of the throne of God.
>
> Hebrews 12:2 RSV

Lord, keep me close to Your heart so that Your joy becomes my strength.

May 13

Once the Lord said to a faithful evangelist, "You have been working for Me with the utmost sincerity for seven years. All that time I have been waiting for the moment that I could start to work through you." The man understood and committed his work totally to the Lord. From that moment on, great blessings started to come on his ministry.

> I am the vine, you are the branches. He who abides in me, and I in him, he it is that bears much fruit, for apart from me you can do nothing.
>
> John 15:5 RSV

Lord, show me how You can work through me. I want to bear much fruit to Your glory. I surrender my work and myself anew into Your hands.

May 14

The Church needs the power and the gifts of the Holy Spirit more now than ever before. The Bible gives special promises.

You shall receive power when the Holy Spirit has come upon you.

Acts 1:8 RSV

Thank You, Lord, that You are willing to use me in the world and in the Church, and that You will give me all the power I need through the Holy Spirit.

May 15

I have a glove here in my hand. The glove cannot do anything by itself, but when my hand is in it, it can do many things. True, it is not the glove, but my hand in the glove that acts. We are gloves. It is the Holy Spirit in us who is the hand, who does the job. We have to make room for the hand so that every finger is filled.

Gracious Spirit, dwell with me; I myself
would gracious be;
And with words that help and heal, would
Thy life in mine reveal;
And with actions bold and meek, would for
Christ my Saviour speak.

Thomas Lynch

For God is at work in you. . . .

Philippians 2:13 RSV

Thank You, Lord, that I am only a glove and the Holy Spirit is the hand in the glove.

May 16

We need to learn not only to be filled with the Holy Spirit but also to stay filled. We do this by becoming sensitive to His work within us. We need to know that the secret of walking in the Spirit is to immediately confess our sins and, by faith, to ask God to refill us.

> . . . how much more will the heavenly Father give the Holy Spirit to those who ask him!
>
> Luke 11:13 RSV

Thank You, Lord, that You have told us, "Be filled with My Spirit." Give us the knowledge that by obeying that command we can live victoriously, to Your honor.

May 17

A lady planned a house meeting, although her brother did not believe it would be successful. The next day she proudly told him her room had been filled with women. The next week she reported that her room had been fuller still, and the third week even fuller.

"Impossible!" her brother said. "When a room is full, it cannot be fuller still."

"Yes," she smiled, "but every week I took out more of my furniture!"

You can be filled with the Holy Spirit, and be still more filled. Perhaps some furniture must be moved out of your heart.

> . . . that Christ will be more and more at home in your hearts.
>
> Ephesians 3:17 LB

Lord, show me if You need more room in my heart for Your Holy Spirit. It is a joy to remove that which could stand in the way.

May 18

People who pray for a revival in the world are truly doing God's work. But in order for a revival to come, there must also be people who are willing to throw themselves totally into the cause of the Gospel.

O Holy Spirit, revival comes from Thee;
Send a revival, start the work in me.
Thy Word declares Thou wilt supply our need;
For blessings now, O Lord, I humbly plead.

J. Edwin Orr

. . . serving the Lord and not men.

Colossians 3:23 RSV

Lord, whatever You choose for me to do, give me the faith and power to do it with all my heart.

May 19

When I was a teenager, my father asked me to visit the women in prison in our town. I would not do it because I was so afraid of prisons! Now, since I have been in prison myself, I have no fear. I even like to speak with prisoners because I know how it feels to be behind a door that can only be opened from the outside. But I also know that with Jesus the worst can happen, the best remains, and His light is stronger than the deepest darkness.

Remember those who are in prison, as though in prison with them; and those who are ill-treated, since you also are in the body.

Hebrews 13:3 RSV

Lord, thank You that You do not give us a spirit of fear but of power, of love, and a sound mind.

May 20

There were three times in my life when prison locks were closed behind me. It was very difficult. Many of us experience locks closed behind us at times when we have almost insurmountable problems. I learned, and you will learn, that that means a difficult class in life's school. But you can learn much, especially when the teacher is able. My teacher was the Lord, and He is willing to be yours.

> Show me Your ways, O Lord; teach me Your paths. Lead me in Your truth, and teach me: for You are the God of my salvation; on You do I wait all the day.
>
> *See* Psalms 25:4, 5 KJV

We are Your willing pupils, Lord. The classroom is of Your choosing, the lessons only part of Your plan for us. Thank You that Your Holy Spirit teaches us how to be willing to study in Your school.

May 21

God Himself is the dynamite of all His demands. God always supplies the power to do all that He requires. We will see more and more that we are chosen not because of our ability but because of His power, which will be demonstrated in our not being able. Jesus was, is, and will be Victor and He is willing to make you and me more than conquerors.

> Thanks be to God, who in Christ always leads us in triumph, and through us spreads the fragrance of the knowledge of him everywhere.
>
> 2 Corinthians 2:14 RSV

Thank You, Lord, for the tremendous reality of Your victory over the problems of today and the problems of tomorrow.

May 22

Brother Andrew wrote me:

I travelled in all the Communist countries. One day I stood in Moscow's Red Square, watching tens of thousands of soldiers marching, singing and shouting, "We are going to conquer the world."

I stood there alone, and would have been scared if I had not known Scripture. I remembered "Greater is he who is in you than he who is in the world." That was a good feeling—one man more than the whole Red Army.

Fear not, for I am with you, be not dismayed, for I am your God; I will strengthen you, I will help you, I will uphold you with my victorious right hand.

Isaiah 41:10 RSV

Hold Thou my hand, so weak I am and helpless
I dare not take one step without Thine aid.
Hold Thou my hand, for then, O loving Saviour,
No dread of ill shall make my soul afraid.

May 23

Gideon was not a very able or strong man, but the Lord was with Gideon, giving him the strength he needed. That is why he was called a mighty man of valor.

And the Lord turned to (Gideon) and said, "Go in this might of yours. . . . "

Judges 6:14 RSV

Thank You, Lord, that because You are with us, we will have power and strength in the battles that lie ahead. With our weak hand in Your strong hand we stand on victory ground. Hallelujah!

May 24

The strength that we claim from God's Word does not depend on circumstances. Circumstances will be difficult, but our strength will be sufficient.

> . . . how tremendous is the power available to us who believe in God.
>
> Ephesians 1:19 Phillips

In good times or in bad, You provide us with the strength we need. It comforts us to have such a reserve available for our use, Father.

May 25

I met a young man who had been a criminal. He told me, "I must go to make restitution. That means I have to go to jail for at least two years."

I asked him, "What must I pray for you?"

"Pray that God protects my quiet time and takes away my fears."

What strength that young man had received from the Lord! How often we refuse to make restitution because it is difficult.

> O Lord, I am Your servant;
> I am Your servant, the son of Your handmaid.
> You have loosed my bonds.
>
> *See* Psalms 116:16 RSV

Lord, what You ask of us may not be pleasant. We ask only that You give us the faith to follow the path You show us, and the power to obey. If it means restitution, I am willing, Lord.

May 26

In ourselves we are not capable of suffering bravely, but the Lord possesses all the strength we lack and will demonstrate His power when we undergo persecution. It makes no difference whether we have great or little power of endurance, or none at all. For Jesus Christ it is the same.

> I will all the more gladly boast of my weaknesses, that the power of Christ may rest upon me.
>
> 2 Corinthians 12:9 RSV

Thank You, Lord, that our strength is not important, for Your strength will be demonstrated even in our weakness.

May 27

Jesus did not promise to change the circumstances around us. He promised great peace and pure joy to those who would learn to believe that God actually controls all things.

> One day, when He shows Himself in full splendour to men, you will be filled with the most tremendous joy. . . . you can be sure that God's Spirit of glory . . . is resting upon you.
>
> 1 Peter 4:13, 14 Phillips

Your will be done, Father. Teach us that You, not we, control our lives for our own good.

May 28

Somebody said to me: "When I worry I go to the mirror and say to myself, 'This tremendous thing which is worrying me is beyond a solution. It is especially too hard for Jesus Christ to handle.' After I have said that, I smile and I am ashamed."

Have no anxiety about anything, but in everything by prayer and supplication with thanksgiving let your requests be made known to God. And the peace of God, which passes all understanding, will keep your hearts and your minds in Christ Jesus.

Philippians 4:6, 7 RSV

Lord, teach me how to smile at my worries. Forgive and cleanse me from my unbelief.

May 29

If a care is too small to be turned into a prayer, it is too small to be made into a burden.

Cast all your cares on God! That anchor holds.

Alfred, Lord Tennyson

Pray at all times in the Spirit, with all prayer and supplication. . . .

Ephesians 6:18 RSV

Remind us that we have the answer to our worries, Father. Give us clear vision about our cares and Your answers.

May 30

We are not called to be burden-bearers, but cross-bearers and light-bearers. We must cast our burdens on the Lord.

Cast your burdens on the Lord,
and he will sustain you;
he will never permit
the righteous to be moved.

Psalms 55:22 RSV

Lord, casting our burdens on You makes it possible for us to go our way with gladness. Thank You.

May 31

We have a Father in heaven who is almighty. Trust Him and you will experience miracles. Is your future a friend this morning? Remember that God is in control.

> Trust in him at all times, O people;
> pour out your heart before him;
> God is a refuge for us. –
>
> Psalms 62:8 RSV

We see Your miracles every day, Father, if we only open our eyes to them.

JUNE

June 1

A missionary wrote me: "Sometimes adversity tempts me to discouragement in the face of seeming failure. But I take courage and press on anew, as I remember that God does not hold me responsible for success, but for faithfulness." Jesus said, "Well done, you faithful servant," not "Well done, you successful servant."

> If any one serves me, he must follow me; and where I am, there shall my servant be also; if any one serves me, the Father will honor him.
>
> John 12:26 RSV

Father, teach us to yield. What You do not have at Your disposal You cannot sanctify, just as the potter cannot form the clay if it is not totally in his hands.

June 2

Conditions are always changing, therefore I must not be dependent upon conditions. What matters supremely is my soul and my relationship to God. God is concerned about me, as my Father. The very hairs of my head are all numbered. Whatever God wills and permits is of necessity for my good.

> Behold, like the clay in the potter's hand, so are you in my hand.
>
> Jeremiah 18:6 RSV

Father, we sometimes argue against Your will, hoping to avoid hardship in our lives, even though it will be for our eventual good. Teach us acceptance.

June 3

A woodpecker tapped with his beak against the stem of a tree just as lightning struck the tree and destroyed it. He flew away and said, "I didn't know there was so much power in my beak!" When we bring the Gospel there is a danger that we will think or say, "I have done a good job." Don't be a silly woodpecker. Know where you strength comes from. It is only the Holy Spirit who can make a message good and fruitful.

It is not *try*, but *trust*. It is not *do*, but *done*.
Our God has planned for us, great victory
    through His Son.

Who can utter the mighty doings of the Lord . . . ?
                        Psalms 106:2 RSV

Holy Spirit, make us jealous for God's honor.

June 4

William Nagenda, the African evangelist, was met at the station by his little three-year-old son. The boy said, "Daddy, I will carry your suitcase." William did not want to disappoint him, so he said, "You lay your hand on my hand," and they carried the suitcase home together. When they reached home, the little boy told his mother, "I carried Daddy's suitcase!"

When we have heavy things to bear, and we overcome by laying our weak hands on the strong hand of the Lord, it is foolish to say, "I have carried the load." We must give the Lord all the honor He is due.

> Abide in me, and I in you. As the branch cannot bear fruit by itself, unless it abides in the vine, neither can you, unless you abide in me.
>
> John 15:4 RSV

Lord, when You give us a load to bear, You give us the strength to carry it. Forgive us if we childishly assume that we have done the work ourselves.

June 5

Oswald Smith told the following illustration about surrender. He took four books in his hand, then laid them down on the altar, one by one.

"This is my money. This is my time. This is my house. This is my family. They are all the Lord's.

"But I have reserved a room for my vacation— that money I will keep for myself." He took back the first book.

"Yes, I gave my time, but that time for my vacation is mine." He took back the second book.

"My house is the Lord's. But my sister is ill and she has six naughty boys. I cannot invite them to my new house. They will make it dirty!" He took back the third book.

"My family is the Lord's. My daughter wanted to become a missionary. That is not possible. She must help her mother." He took back the fourth book.

After I heard that story, I saw that in my life I had taken back that which I had first surrendered. I dedicated my life anew to the Lord. We must do that time and time again. (I experienced that surely the Lord gives vacations, but when we take them from His hand, and not as our right, they become a blessing to those we travel with and meet on vacation.)

You are not your own, you were bought with a price.
1 Corinthians 6:19, 20 RSV

Take my life, and let it be consecrated, Lord, to Thee.

June 6

A rich businessman told me that he had surrendered to the Lord. I asked him, "Did you surrender one hundred percent?"

"No, only ninety-five percent. I have to abide by other men's decisions in my work," he replied.

"Have you ever looked death in the eye?"

"Yes. During the war."

"Did you surrender one hundred percent then?"

"Yes!"

"But you are standing just as much in the face of death now. It can come at any moment. Every human being knows that he must die some time and it could be today. Surrender one hundred percent!"

What a safety in life and death, to belong to Jesus Christ, lock, stock, and barrel!

When our Captain bids us "Go,"
It is not ours to murmur "No."
He that gives the sword and shield,
Chooses too the battlefield
On which we are to fight the foe.

I will praise thee, O Lord, among the people: and I will sing praises unto thee among the nations.
Psalms 108:3 KJV

Lord Jesus Christ, Your wishes above ours, Your commands above the world's, Your glory above all glories, now and forever.

June 7

The Bible is indestructible. Voltaire expected that within fifty years of his lifetime there would not be one Bible in the world. His house is now a distribution center for Bibles in many languages.

Heaven and earth will pass away, but my words will not pass away.

Mark 13:31 RSV

Such a treasure will never fade or dim. It will be available for our children's children. We thank You for this precious legacy, Father.

June 8

Divine guidance is for all God's children who ask to be guided. Submit to Him if you should be tempted by your own human desires. Guidance does not come automatically. Receiving guidance is a skill to be learned, not a method. It is intensely personal.

It is these things that we talk about, not using the expressions of the human intellect but those which the Holy Spirit teaches us. . . .

1 Corinthians 2:13 Phillips

Lord, teach me how to receive Your guidance. Make me aware of Your gentle direction in my life.
Lord, teach me how to receive Your guidance. Make me aware of Your gentle direction in my life.

June 9

As you submit to God's guidance, you will find that He has taken the incentive in your life, adjusting and rearranging where you have been off the track. You will never find His demands to be greater than that which you can accomplish in His power.

> I was not ever thus, nor prayed that Thou
>   shouldst lead me on;
> I loved to choose and see my path; but now
>   lead Thou me on.
>
> John H. Newman

Where there is no guidance, a people falls. . . .
Proverbs 11:14 RSV

Father, forgive my past willfulness and be my guide.

June 10

Much of what we do through our own strength has to be cleansed, but that which we do through the Lord has value for time and eternity.

When Jesus takes your hand, He keeps you close. When Jesus keeps you close, He leads you through life. When Jesus leads you through life, He brings you safely home.

Casper Ten Boom

Preserve me, O God, for in thee I take refuge.
Psalms 16:1 RSV

Keep me safe in Your hands, Lord Jesus, guiding me in all I do for Your honor.

June 11

Direct interference from God is usually for the purpose of adjusting or correcting the way of His children. Much as a space scientist would make an in-flight course correction on a rocket speeding toward the moon, God's guidance is so natural that the Spirit-led Christian will hardly be aware of it. Often in the eternal counsel of God, it has operated before we made the discovery.

Teach me Your way, O Lord;
and lead me on a level path. . . .
See Psalms 27:11 RSV

Father, show us the way to go with our lives. Direct us, even if we are unaware of Your influence on our decisions.

June 12

The admission of commitment to God resembles getting on an airplane. Once you are on board, you don't worry about the directions, for they are the pilot's job. Your responsibility is to get on the right airplane and, where necessary, to change planes. The pilot must do the guiding and the pilot is the Holy Spirit.

I am the Lord your God,
who teaches you to profit,
who leads you in the way you should go.
Isaiah 48:17 RSV

Father, thank You that the Holy Spirit controls my life, leading me in the path You choose for me to travel.

June 13

Sincerity is not guidance. Sincerity may say, "I am sure this plane goes to New York." You believe this sincerely, but the plane will go to Miami if it is scheduled for Miami, and your sincerity will do nothing to change that!

There is a way which seems right to a man,
but its end is the way to death.

Proverbs 14:12 RSV

Father, we often sincerely believe we are doing right, even if we are wrong. Give us wisdom through Your Holy Spirit. Guide us so that we do Your will, not ours.

June 14

Do you try to lead a godly life through your own efforts, and wonder why you so often fail? Can a broom stand on its own? No, it must be held up, or lean on something.

So it is with us. We can no more stand on our own than a broom can. It is necessary to surrender to the only One who can keep us upright.

Now to him who is able to keep you from falling and to present you without blemish before the presence of his glory with rejoicing, to the only God, our Savior through Jesus Christ our Lord, be glory, majesty, dominion, and authority, before all time and now and for ever. Amen.

Jude 24, 25 RSV

By ourselves we are floored, Lord. Thank You that You are our support and guide.

June 15

When God measures a man, He puts the tape measure around his heart, not his head.

> ... the Lord sees not as man sees; man looks on the outward appearance, but the Lord looks on the heart.
>
> 1 Samuel 16:7 RSV

Lord, what a joy that You do not see as man sees and that Your measuring is perfect.

June 16

We cannot trust ourselves to do the right thing. We may become too smug on one side, or too despairing on the other. Trust only in the Lord for your guidance.

> All to Jesus I surrender.
> Make me, Saviour, wholly Thine;
> Let me feel the Holy Spirit,
> Truly know that Thou art mine.
> All to Jesus I surrender;
> Lord I give myself to Thee.
> Fill me with Thy love and power;
> Let Thy blessing fall on me.
>
> J. W. Van Deventer

> ... that ye may abound in hope through the power of the Holy Ghost.
>
> Romans 15:13 KJV

Lord, what joy to know that I am within the boundary where Your love can reach and comfort me. Your will is perfect; mine is flawed. Lead me into perfect obedience of Your perfect will.

June 17

Take the far look often. Looking up is healthier for the eyes than looking down. God's promises are like a home hearth fire by which we may warm our hearts and our hands.

> And the marvellous thing is this, that we now receive not the spirit of the world but the Spirit of God Himself, so that we can actually understand something of God's generosity towards us.
>
> 1 Corinthians 2:12 Phillips

Father, thank You for Your promises which light our way and make plain our part in Your plan.

June 18

A dying man said, "I cannot remember a single promise, but that does not matter. God does not forget any."

> As you live this new life, we pray that you will be strengthened from God's boundless resources, so that you will find yourselves able to pass through any experience and endure it with courage.
>
> Colossians 1:11 Phillips

Thanks be to You, Lord, that Your promises endure forever.

June 19

Let the Bible speak. Use the full appeal of the Scriptures, even though the people who listen do not believe. In witnessing, our primary function is proclamation, not defense.

> My tongue shall speak of thy word.
>
> Psalms 119:172 KJV

Father, help us to speak with authority, the authority of Your Word.

June 20

The Body of Christ is suffering much persecution. More than 60 percent of the Christians in the world are in tribulation. If you are a Christian then you have to share their problems and help them by your intercession, and wherever possible write to them and assist those who help them. Watchman Nee said, "When my feet were beaten, my hands suffered pain." In a practical way we must sympathize with those who are suffering and sustain them with our prayers.

> Therefore we ourselves boast of you in the churches of God for your steadfastness and faith in all your persecutions and in the afflictions which you are enduring.
>
> 2 Thessalonians 1:4 RSV

When one of us suffers for You, we all suffer, Lord, for we are all one in the Body of Christ. We share pain as we share glory.

June 21

Are you ready to suffer for Him who suffered so much for you? Are you willing to be obedient? He intends to use your suffering to make you worthy of His Kingdom. We are citizens of heaven. Our outlook goes beyond this world.

> I consider that the sufferings of this present time are not worth comparing with the glory that is to be revealed to us.
>
> Romans 8:18 RSV

Lord Jesus, You are the Victor. We thank You for the joy of being called by such a loving and powerful King of kings!

June 22

I found that when some Russians who were in great tribulation and persecution heard that we were willing to pray for them, they never said, "Pray that God will stop this persecution." They said, "Pray that God will give us the strength to suffer for Him."

> ... you have shown such endurance and faith in all the trials and persecutions you have gone through.... He intends to use your suffering to make you worthy of His Kingdom....
>
> 2 Thessalonians 1:4, 5 Phillips

Lord Jesus, You suffered for me—what am I suffering for You?

June 23

In the concentration camp we went through the ordeal of being stripped of all our clothing and made to stand naked for several hours. It was more difficult, more cruel, than anything else we experienced.

As I stood there, it was suddenly as if I saw Jesus at the cross. The Bible tells us they took away His garments and He hung there naked. Through my suffering, I understood a fraction of the suffering of Jesus, and it made me so happy and thankful that I could bear my suffering. "Love so amazing, so divine, demands of my soul, my life, my all." (Isaac Watts).

> And they crucified him....
>
> Matthew 27:35 KJV

Father, when we have to suffer, show us Jesus at the cross.

June 24

I was watching the actors during the filming of *The Hiding Place.* The women who came out of the prison gate looked tired and cold. Then I saw the woman who was playing Corrie ten Boom. There I was, sitting and looking at my own story! Suddenly it was too much. I could not keep my tears back any longer. But through that a deep wound was healed. I knew why I had had that time of suffering. I learned a lesson that I could share with many people the world over.

Our little inch of time of suffering is not worthy of our first night's welcome home to Heaven.

Samuel Rutherford

(Jesus said) "... you will be with me in Paradise."
Luke 23:43 RSV

Thank You, Lord Jesus, for what You have suffered for us at the cross, for all our sins.

June 25

Live your lives in love, the same sort of love which Christ gives us, and which He perfectly expressed when He gave Himself as a sacrifice to God. Love is not soft as water is; it is solid as a rock on which the waves of hatred beat in vain.

Love ... is, in fact, the one thing that still stands when all else has fallen.
1 Corinthians 13:8 Phillips

Thank You, Lord, that we have an eternity in which to thank and praise You for Your love.

June 26

There are two kinds of love—human love and God's love. God's love never fails, but human love does. God demonstrates His love to the world through us.

> Herein is love, not that we loved God, but that he loved us, and sent his Son to be the propitiation for our sins.
>
> 1 John 4:10 KJV

Lord, I am willing to act in love toward others. Make me a small reflection of Your love, for even a small reflection can bring light into a dark corner. Thank You!

June 27

Betsie's sleeping place beside me in prison was empty. She had just died. I motioned to a newly arrived Russian prisoner who was looking for a place to sleep, and she gratefully joined me.

We were sharing the same pillow, and with our faces so close, I wanted to speak. But I did not know her language.

"*Jezus Christus?*" I asked softly.

"Oh!" she exclaimed. Quickly making the sign of the cross, she threw her arms around me.

She who had been my sister for fifty-two years had left me. A Russian woman now claimed my love. And there would be others, too, who would be my sisters and brothers in Christ all around the world.

> Truly, I say to you, there is no man who has left house or wife or brothers or parents or children, for the sake of the kingdom of God, who will not

receive manifold more in this time, and in the age
to come eternal life.

Luke 18:29, 30 RSV

Lord, when we accepted You as our Saviour, You
welcomed us into a worldwide family, filled with
loving brothers and sisters. Thank You for this gift
of fellowship.

June 28

God makes us welcome in the everlasting love
He bears for His Son. Did you ever doubt your love
for God? I doubted mine. Did you ever doubt God's
love for His Son? Never! You and I are made welcome in that love. What joy! What riches!

> O love of God, how deep and great
> Far deeper than man's deepest hate.
> Uncomprehended and unbought
> Beyond all knowledge and all thought.

And walk in love, as Christ loved us. . . .

Ephesians 5:2 RSV

Lord, we thank You and praise Your name for Your
welcome! How unspeakably great it is!

June 29

A bird does not know it can fly before it uses
its wings. We learn God's love in our hearts as soon
as we act upon it.

> Though we have never yet seen God, when we love
> each other God lives in us and his love within us
> grows ever stronger.

1 John 4:12 LB

Thank You, Lord Jesus, that You have brought into
our hearts God's love through the Holy Spirit who
is given to us.

June 30

When I was a little girl, my father used to tuck me into bed at night. He talked with me, prayed with me, and laid his big hand on my little face. I did not move because I wanted to keep the feeling of that big hand on my face. It was a comfort to me.

Later, when I was in the concentration camp, I would sometimes pray, "My heavenly Father, will you lay Your hand on my face?" That would bring me peace, and I would be able to sleep. Because father showed me his fatherly love, I could later understand the heavenly Father's love. Fathers and mothers, show your children your love.

I have loved you with an everlasting love. . . .
Jeremiah 31:3 RSV

Our Father, if we are parents or grandparents, help us to reflect Your love to our children and grandchildren to train them in trusting their earthly protectors so that they can find the way when they need their heavenly Father's help.

JULY

July 1

The highest potential of God's love and power is available for us in the trivial things of everyday life.

> Can men tell that you love Jesus?
> Can they, by your life and mine,
> See in daily walk and action
> That we have His life divine?

> ... Our Father, which art in heaven, Hallowed be thy name.
> > Matthew 6:9 KJV

Lord, show us today in everything we experience that we are dependent children of a loving heavenly Father.

July 2

The riches promised in the Bible are difficult to describe because they are earthly reproductions of heavenly riches. Therefore the Bible authors used what I call the "uns":

> Unfathomable—His wondrous love
> Unchangeable—His ways
> Unsearchable—His blessed truths
> Unutterable—His praise
> Unimaginable—His splendor
> Unspeakable—His joy and gifts
> Unnumbered—His company of angels

O the depth of the riches and wisdom and knowledge of God! How unsearchable are his judgments and how inscrutable his ways!

Romans 11:33 RSV

Lord, frankly I stand amazed at the unfathomable complexity of Your wisdom and Your knowledge. How could men ever understand Your reasons for Your actions or explain Your method of working?

July 3

It never ceases to amaze me the way the Lord creates a bond among believers which reaches across continents, beyond race and color.

This is my commandment, that you love one another as I have loved you.

John 15:12 RSV

Father, we declare our oneness with Your children all over the world. Thank You for our fellowship together. It is a little foretaste of heaven.

July 4

Early Christians traced the outline of a fish on their homes, tombs, and catacombs to identify themselves to each other. The fish was used because the Greek word for fish was a simple code in which each letter stood for another word. The five letters stood for the words *Jesus Christ, God's Son, Saviour.*

> Every knee shall bow to Jesus,
> Every tongue confess His name.
> Every knee shall bow to Jesus,
> Here with joy, or there with shame.
> Bow to Jesus, bow to Jesus,
> Bow your heart to Jesus now.

And he is the head of the body, the church. . . .

Colossians 1:18 KJV

How wonderful to be in the company of Your people, Lord, and all the others who have gone before us as Your servants!

July 5

An East German border guard once detained me in his office for three hours. He questioned me thoroughly about my work, but as time went by, I could feel him softening. I was impatient at the delay, knowing I had work to do in his country, but I used the time to try to bring him and his secretary to the Lord. Just before he passed me through, they both accepted books from me. As I left, he explained, "I am sorry to have delayed you, but what we have been doing here is more important than your visit to your friends." The Lord had used those three hours to bring His Good News to two people who walked in the darkness, and I had been impatient!

. . . I seek not my own will but the will of him who sent me.

John 5:30 RSV

Even delays and detours come from You, Lord, and serve Your purpose, when we serve as a channel between You and people we meet. Keep us from impatience. Don't let us pass by people who need Your Word.

July 6

Let us remember that God's Word stands forever, and His commandments mean the same for us today as for His disciples two thousand years ago. Those who act on them in obedience will in the same way prove God's almighty power.

All who keep his commandments abide in him, and he in them.

1 John 3:24 RSV

We obey Your laws with joy, Father. Our eagerness to do so comes not from fear but from love. You give us so much and You ask so little in return.

July 7

When God tells me to visit a country, I obey His direction. So when I saw that a clerk in a travel agency had changed my route, I telephoned her back immediately.

"Why must I go from Sydney to Tel Aviv and then to Cape Town, instead of from Sydney to Cape Town?"

"I am sorry, but there is no refueling spot in the Indian Ocean."

"Well, I cannot change my plans. I will just have to pray for an island!"

In only a few minutes' time she telephoned me again, saying she had received a telegram from Qantas (the Australian airline) announcing that they had arranged a refueling place in the Cocos Islands so that there was now a direct flight from Sydney to Cape Town.

Trust in the Lord with all your heart,
and do not rely on your own insight.
Proverbs 3:5 RSV

Trusting in You brings us in the territory of miracles, Father. It is so good to know that You do not make mistakes when You make Your plans for us.

July 8

When I saw Sadhu Sundar Singh in Europe, he had completed a tour around the world. People asked him, "Doesn't it do harm, your getting so much honor?"

The Sadhu's answer was: "No. The donkey went into Jerusalem, and they put garments on the ground before him. He was not proud. He knew it was not done to honor him, but for Jesus, who was sitting on his back. When people honor me, I know it is not me, but the Lord, who does the job."

> Worthy art thou, our Lord and God,
> to receive glory and honor and power,
> for thou didst create all things,
> and by thy will they existed and were created.
> Revelation 4:11 RSV

Lord, when men honor us for our works, we know that the honor is truly Yours.

July 9

Let us pray that God will send workers to the harvest fields. They look very ripe. Maybe you are the one who needs to go. Be obedient and follow the Lord's call. You will never experience real joy if you don't do the will of the Father. And don't forget that the Lord specializes in the impossible. In the center of His will is peace. Ask the Lord's guidance in obedience. It is possible that where you are now in your home, your office, your job, is the mission field where the harvest has to be reaped. It could be He wants you farther afield. Ask Him what His will is.

> May the God of peace . . . equip you with everything good that you may do his will. . . .
> Hebrews 13:20, 21 RSV

Thank You, Lord, for Your perfect plan for my life. Make me willing to be made willing to do what You tell me to do.

July 10

There is a hunger in our hearts that is never satisfied, except by Jesus. Do you feel lonesome and hungry? Do you have problems that you can't solve? Do you feel chased, with no way out? Come to Him.

> May the God of hope fill you with all joy and peace in believing, so that by the power of the Holy Spirit you may abound in hope.
>
> Romans 15:13 RSV

Jesus, thank You that because of Your constant presence, I am never alone. Hold my hand tightly, Lord. Although afflictions may torment me, they can never defeat me.

July 11

We are moons. God is our sun. If the world comes between the moon and the sun, it is dark. The insecurity of the world is meant to be the raw material of our faith. Surrender to the enemy means death, but surrender to Jesus means life. Confess, commit, claim His presence.

> ... be blameless and innocent, children of God without blemish in the midst of a crooked and perverse generation, among whom you shine as lights in the world.
>
> Philippians 2:15 RSV

Lord Jesus, thank You for Your grace. The world grows more fearsome, but You are our salvation.

July 12

Jesus is able to untangle all the snarls in your soul and to banish all complexes. He will transform even your fixed habit patterns, no matter how deeply they are etched in your subconsciousness.

> If any of you lack wisdom, let him ask God, who gives to all men generously and without reproaching, and it will be given him.
>
> James 1:5 RSV

We have habits we think we cannot break, attitudes we cannot change. Give us the sense to ask for Your answer, Lord.

July 13

It is a joy that God never abandons His children. He guides faithfully all who listen to His directions.

> Guide me, O Thou great Jehovah,
> Pilgrim through this barren land.
> I am weak, but Thou art mighty,
> Hold me with Thy powerful hand.
>
> William Williams

> . . . his truth endureth to all generations.
>
> Psalms 100:5 KJV

Lord, make us ever ready to do Your will and not our own. Your power is ours to use when we follow Your guidance. What a comfort!

July 14

Through the blood of Christ we are inside the circle of God's love and purpose, for Christ is our living peace.

> Stay always within the boundaries where God's love can reach and bless you.
>
> Jude 21 LB

We count everything as loss, compared with the priceless privilege, overwhelming preciousness, surpassing worth, supreme advantage, of knowing You, Lord Jesus. We are progressively more deeply and intimately becoming acquainted with You. Hallelujah!

July 15

So many times we wonder why God allows certain things to happen to us. We try to understand the circumstances of our lives, and are left wondering. But the Holy Spirit shows us that God does not make mistakes.

> The foolishness of God is wiser than men, and the weakness of God is stronger than men.
>
> 1 Corinthians 1:25 RSV

We cannot begin to understand Your aims, Father, and without that understanding our lives often seem to be a great maze. But we know You see the end of the path, and we trust You to guide us through all the turns and blind alleys.

July 16

Whenever you come in contact with mentally retarded people, please tell them that God loves them. They can often enjoy God's love better than people who have problems because of intellectual doubt.

> Has not God made the wisdom of this world look foolish? For it was after the world in its wisdom had failed to know God, that He in His Wisdom chose to save all who would believe by the "simplemindedness" of the Gospel message.
>
> 1 Corinthians 1:20, 21 Phillips

Lord, give us the courage to speak the truth simply, so all can understand. Some will ridicule our lack of sophisticated thinking, so we will need Your courage to remain simple. But we know that Your "foolishness" is wiser than the wisdom of men.

July 17

The greatest thing one person can do for another is to pray for him. Prayer wins the victories; any other service we perform is simply reaping the results of prayer.

> Pray at all times in the Spirit, with all prayer supplication.
>
> Ephesians 6:18 RSV

Father, we can personally reach so few people, but through prayer You have allowed us to help even those whom we will never see here on earth. Thank You for this important means of accomplishing Your work.

July 18

A mother saw her little boy sitting in a corner of the room, saying, "ABCDEFG."

"What are you doing?" she asked.

"Mom, you told me I should pray, but I have never prayed in my life and I don't know how. So I gave God the whole alphabet and asked Him to make a good prayer out of it."

That boy understood a little bit of what Paul says in Romans 8:26—that the Holy Spirit Himself helps us to pray. Yes, He prays in us.

> . . . we do not know how to pray as we ought, but the Spirit himself intercedes for us with sighs too deep for words.
>
> Romans 8:26 RSV

Lord, what a joy that You do the job and together with You we are able to pray and to live for Your honor.

July 19

What wings are to a bird, and sails to a ship, is prayer to the soul.

> We mutter, we sputter—
> We fume and we spurt.
> We mumble and grumble—
> Our feelings get hurt.
> We can't understand things—
> Our vision gets dim,
> When all that we need—
> Is a moment with Him.

. . . men ought always to pray, and not to faint.

Luke 18:1

Thank You, Lord, that we may, that we must, pray.

July 20

Prayer should never be an excuse for inaction. Nehemiah prayed, but he also set watches for protection—he used common sense. As a result, what had not been done in a hundred years' time was finished in fifty-two days.

So the wall was finished . . . in fifty-two days.

Nehemiah 6:15 RSV

Holy Spirit, we claim wisdom from You especially when we do not see the clear pattern of praying and acting.

July 21

Following completion of the wall, a great revival came to Jerusalem. The power of one man, Nehemiah, living in fellowship with God, was well used. Today's greatest need is for people who live in fellowship with God.

> The God of heaven will make us prosper, and we his servants will arise and build. . . .
>
> Nehemiah 2:20 RSV

Father, our powers are limited until we come close to You. Once we do that, we can do anything You require of us.

July 22

My father said to me several times, "My name is on my watchmaker's business, but God's name really should be on the shop. I am a watchmaker by the grace of God." I know that my father was a Christian first and a businessman second.

> By the grace of God I am what I am, and his grace toward me was not in vain. On the contrary, I worked harder than any of them, though it was not I, but the grace of God which is with me.
>
> 1 Corinthians 15:10 RSV

Lord, what a joy and security that I belong to You with all that I am and possess in my work and everyday life.

July 23

When I was a little girl I was sure that Jesus was a member of the ten Boom family. It was just as easy to talk to Him as it was to carry on a conversation with my mother and father. Jesus was there. I was closer to the reality and truth of Jesus' presence than the one who makes fellowship with the Lord a problem by his reasoning and logical thinking.

> Where two or three are gathered in my name, there am I in the midst of them.
>
> Matthew 18:20 RSV

Lord, how wonderful to be Your friend, to feel You close to us every hour, and to know Your love for us never fades.

July 24

Father and Mother lived on the edge of poverty, and yet their contentment was not dependent upon their surroundings. Their relationship to each other and to the Lord gave them strength and happiness.

> God is our refuge and strength, a very present help in trouble.
>
> Psalms 46:1 RSV

Lord Jesus, with You close, what else do we really need? With Your love, we have the best; without Your love, we are truly poor, whatever our circumstances.

July 25

When Papa took a watch apart to repair it and put it back together again, it was a task he performed without regard to the owner's social status or wealth. He taught us that it is more important what God thinks of the job you have done than what you yourself think, or what other people think.

> . . . obey in everything those who are your earthly masters, not with eyeservice, as men-pleasers, but in singleness of heart, fearing the Lord. What-

ever your task, work heartily, as serving the Lord
and not men.

Colossians 3:22, 23 RSV

Lord Jesus, what a joy that when You enter into
our lives, even the smallest actions are important.
We may claim Your discipline and victory in the
work of everyday life.

July 26

God gives us two types of guidance. The first
is unconscious, and comes because our lives are
committed to Jesus. The second is special guidance,
for instance when God wants to move us in a new
direction—a new job or a new field of work.

I will instruct you and teach you
the way you should go;
I will counsel you with my eye upon you.

Psalms 32:8 RSV

We need Your wisdom in our lives, Father. Help us
to know Your will so that we can make those few
large decisions that alter our lives from time to time.

July 27

We must not make our own plans without God's
guidance. Do your planning while in prayer. Be
sure that the Lord is walking before you and that
you are not recklessly rushing ahead of Him.

He leadeth me! Oh, blessed thought!
Oh, words with heavenly comfort fraught.
Whate'er I do, where'er I be,
Still 'tis God's hand that leadeth me.

Joseph H. Gilmore

And the Lord shall guide thee continually . . .

Isaiah 58:11

Lord, give us patience to wait for Your guidance. Keep us from rash actions, no matter how right they seem at the time.

July 28

While visiting NORAD in Colorado, I talked to a general. He had a walkie-talkie, and told me that he had "over the horizon radar contact" with the president and other strategic points twenty-four hours a day.

And I thought, I, too, have "over the horizon radar contact," through the Holy Spirit. I have contact with my heavenly Father, and I know my strategic points.

> We can only see a little of God's loving,
> A few rich samples of His mighty store.
> But out there, beyond the eye's horizon,
> There is more, there is more.

... Fear not ... I am thy shield, and thy exceeding great reward.   Genesis 15:1

Thank You, Lord. We have no need to fear when the Holy Spirit is with us as our protector and guide.

July 29

Before the war I was a watchmaker. When my hand was not steady and I had to do a very exact piece of work on a watch, I would pray, "Lord Jesus, will You lay Your hand on my hand?" He always did, and our joined hands worked firmly and securely.

Jesus never fails us for a moment.

And the hand of the Lord was with them. . . .
     Acts 11:21 RSV

Remind us that You are always with us, Lord. Thank You that even our smallest problems concern You. You answer our slightest need.

July 30

Jesus paid all your sin bills on the cross. Claim the riches that are yours through Him. Live as a child of the King, not as a beggar!

> He has granted to us his precious and very great promises, that through these you may escape from the corruption that is in the world because of passion, and become partakers of the divine nature.
>
> 2 Peter 1:4 RSV

Thank You, Lord Jesus, that You have freed us from sin and unlocked a treasure chest of grace for our use. Our riches are greater than all the earth's gold and silver combined!

July 31

Don't ask, "Can I be kept from sin, if I keep close to Him?" Ask instead, "Can I be kept from sin, if He is near me?" Then you will see how reliable He is. Confess, humble yourself, admit what you have done. Keep the door closed to sin through the blood of Jesus and in the name of Jesus.

> False Christs and false prophets will arise and show great signs and wonders, so as to lead astray, if possible, even the elect.
>
> Matthew 24:24 RSV

We are so glad it is written, "*if* possible," Lord! What a joy that it is not possible and that it is You Yourself who prepares us and gives us the grace and discernment we need.

AUGUST

August 1

The American astronauts who went to the moon had to be in constant contact with their leader. When the contact was broken, they did nothing else until it was restored. When your connection with God is broken because of sin, you must do what His Word says to restore that connection.

> My little children, I am telling you this so that you will stay away from sin. But if you sin, there is someone to plead for you before the Father. His name is Jesus Christ. . . .
>
> 1 John 2:1 LB

> If we confess our sins to him, he can be depended on to forgive us and to cleanse us from every wrong.
>
> 1 John 1:9 LB

Thank You, Lord Jesus, that You restore all broken contact when we come to You with our sins.

August 2

I often looked death in the eye when I was a prisoner. When I saw the smoke go up from the crematorium I asked myself, "When will it be my turn to be killed?" I did not know that one week before they killed all the women my age I would be set free through a miracle of God and a blunder in the administration. When you look at death you see everything in such an uncomplicated way. I saw that the devil was strong, much stronger than I, but then I looked at Jesus. He was strong, much stronger than the devil. Together with Him, I was much stronger than the devil.

Thanks be to God, who gives us the victory through our Lord Jesus Christ.

1 Corinthians 15:57 RSV

Lord Jesus, thank You that when we are yokefellows with You, we stand on victory ground. Hallelujah!

August 3

Today is the day of salvation. Some people miss heaven by only eighteen inches—the distance between their heads and their hearts. One of the devil's most successful wiles is "Wait awhile." But we need to listen to God.

For man believes with his heart and so is justified, and he confesses with his lips and so is saved.

Romans 10:10 RSV

Lord, if You are not yet in my heart, but only in my head, please come down to my heart. Fill it with Your life, through Your grace. Thank You, Lord Jesus.

August 4

Sometimes the devil speaks of our sins and makes us despair. He takes away our courage. He tells us, "You will be that way all of your life. There is no hope for you!" The devil is a liar! We are what we are in Jesus Christ.

At the Cross, at the Cross,
Where I first saw the light,

And the burden of my heart rolled away,
It was there by faith I received my sight. . . .
Ralph E. Hudson

I thank my God . . . for the grace of God which is
given you by Jesus Christ.
1 Corinthians 1:4 KJV

Thank You for Your gift of grace and peace, Lord.
When we know we are forgiven we have victory
and joy, despite what the devil says.

August 5

Sin can break your connection with God. The
great joy is that we know the Bible has the answer
for that problem! When we confess our sins, the
Lord is faithful and forgives us.

I have swept away your transgressions like a cloud,
and your sins like mist. . . .
Isaiah 44:22 RSV

Thank You, Lord Jesus, for that blessed answer to
my sin problem: the cross, where You finished all
that was necessary in order to destroy my sin. Keep
me close to You, Lord, so that I see Your amazing
grace.

August 6

Are you honest? Go to your bookshelf, check
which books you have borrowed, and send them
back. You may not steal.

. . . you will need the strong belt of truth. . . .
See Ephesians 6:14 LB

Lord, Thank You that we have the spiritual armor
of Ephesians 6, and can stand victorious against
"decent" and "indecent" sins.

August 7

The riches of the Bible are ours, but people continue to argue over interpretation. For those who have not yet accepted the Saviour Jesus Christ, and who are therefore lost, it is the same as having your house on fire, and then having to listen to the firemen argue about which hose to use!

> ...who are you to criticise the servant of somebody else, especially when that Somebody Else is God? It is to his own Master that he gives, or fails to give, satisfactory service. And don't doubt that satisfaction, for God is well able to transform men into servants who are satisfactory.
>
> Romans 14:3, 4 Phillips

Lord, we know it is not our place to decide who is right and who is wrong in any matter. Your promises are there for our salvation, not for our discussion.

August 8

Does being born into a Christian family make one a Christian? No! God has no grandchildren. Each person must make the decision for the Lord himself.

> Unless one is born anew, he cannot see the kingdom of God.
>
> John 3:3 RSV

Lord, give us much wisdom to teach our children Your Word, so that when You come to them, they will be eagerly waiting.

August 9

Here is a prayer which one could use for somebody who wants to come to the Lord: Jesus, I ask

You to come into my life. I am a sinner. I have been trusting myself and my own good works, but now I put my trust in You. I accept You as my own personal Saviour. I believe You died for me. I receive You as Lord and Master over my life. Help me to turn from my sins and to follow You. I accept Your forgiveness and Your gift of eternal life. I thank You for it. Amen.

> God so loved the world that he gave his only Son, that whoever believes in him should not perish but have eternal life.
>
> John 3:16 RSV

Prayer of the counselor: Lord Jesus, You have heard this prayer. Once You said, "Those who come to Me I will in no wise cast out!" Lord, what a welcome! I ask You that Your Holy Spirit will give to this person the assurance of life eternal. Bless him with the certainty that his sins are forgiven. Thank You.

August 10

"Thank you so much, Corrie," a woman told me one day after I had shown her the way of salvation and challenged her to make a decision for Jesus.

"How impolite you are!" I answered. "Someone knocks, and instead of talking with Him, you say thank you to me. Jesus asked you something."

We had a conversation together. At last she said, "Oh, I see! Forgive me, Lord Jesus. Yes, come into my heart." He came.

"Talk with Him," I said. "Admit whatever sins He has found, and repent. *Now* you may thank me!"

> But thanks be to God, who gives us the victory through our Lord Jesus Christ.
>
> 1 Corinthians 15:57 RSV

Lord, keep us mindful that as Your messengers we are not important. It is Your message that matters.

August 11

One day when I was five years old, my mother watched me playing house. She saw me knock on an imaginary neighbor's door and wait for an answer.

"Corrie," she said, "I know Someone who is standing at your door and knocking. He is Jesus. Would you like to invite Him into your heart?"

I said yes, I wanted Jesus in my heart. She put her hand in mine, and we prayed together.

Does a young child understand spiritual matters? I know Jesus became more real to me from that day on. Children need to be led, not left to wander.

Train up a child in the way he should go,
and when he is old he will not depart from it.

Proverbs 22:6 RSV

Lord, give me an opportunity to bring my child to You today. I know that is the greatest gift I can give him.

August 12

We are ministers of Christ. Stewardship of the mysteries of God has been entrusted to us. Be a faithful steward.

This is how one should regard us, as servants of Christ and stewards of the mysteries of God. Moreover it is required of stewards that they be found trustworthy.

1 Corinthians 4:1, 2 RSV

Here I am, Lord. I have accepted Your promises to make me a steward. Thank You for Your grace and my salvation. Take my life and use me.

August 13

Peter said, "No, Lord!" But he had to learn that one cannot say no while saying "Lord" and that one cannot say "Lord" while saying no.

Obey my voice, and I will be your God, and you shall be my people.

Jeremiah 7:23 RSV

Lord, make me responsive to Your will. I know that then I can lead a victorious life to Your honor.

August 14

As a camel kneels before his master to have him remove his burden at the end of the day, so kneel each night and let the Master take your burden.

Cast your burden on the Lord,
and he will sustain you;
he will never permit
the righteous to be moved.

Psalms 55:22 RSV

Lord, take our daily burdens from us so that we will be refreshed and strong for the next day's journey.

August 15

God's ways are sometimes not understandable. He led the Jews around the land of the Philistines, although it was shorter to pass through that land.

For my thoughts are not your thoughts,
neither are your ways my ways, says the Lord.

Isaiah 55:8 RSV

Father, when we question Your ways, help us to remember that we do not need to understand completely, but that it is sufficient that we obey.

August 16

Before she died in the concentration camp, my sister Betsie was inspired by the Lord to show me the work I would do after the war.

When I had to leave that work I felt very sad. I even became depressed, until somebody showed me that bondage to someone who has died is wrong. I was set free and the Lord gave me great peace.

> For freedom Christ has set us free; stand fast therefore. . . .
>
> Galatians 5:1 RSV

Lord, the wishes of those we love are a pleasant bondage, but only as long as they do not keep us from doing Your work. Help us to break bonds that must be broken.

August 17

Missed opportunities!

If only . . .

It is good to regret missed opportunities, but quite wrong to be miserable about them. You cannot look back across your past life without seeing things to regret. That is as it should be. But we have to draw a subtle distinction between a legitimate regret and a wrong condition of heart. Give God your "if onlies."

Think of those laborers in the vineyard in the parable which Jesus told in Matthew 20:1-16. They all received the same wages, although some had worked the whole day and some had worked for only an hour. Compare that to a person's life. Some people enter the Kingdom right at the end of their lives. They may regret all those years when they were not serving Christ. But the important thing is that they are in the Kingdom. The thing that matters first of all, if you are a Christian, is not what you once were but what you are now.

I will restore to you the years
which the swarming locust has eaten. . . .
Joel 2:25 RSV

Lord Jesus, I give my "if onlies" to You. Make me a faithful laborer here and now.

August 18

How can Jesus trust us to spread His Word? Because He has given us the Holy Spirit and the Bible; they are all we will need.

To me, though I am the very least of all the saints, this grace was given, to preach to the Gentiles the unsearchable riches of Christ.
Ephesians 3:8 RSV

Father, Thank You for providing Your army with all the supplies it needs. Even the weakest soldier becomes powerful if he has the right equipment.

August 19

During my first visit to Japan, by mistake I asked a non-Christian to close a meeting with prayer. He admitted that he was not a Christian, so I said the prayer myself. After the meeting he came to me to explain why he could not pray. Now I had a chance to have a fruitful talk with him and he accepted the Lord Jesus. Do you see? My blunder of mistaking one man for another had been used to give me the opportunity to bring that man to Jesus! God has no problems, only plans.

> . . . freely forgiven through that full and generous grace. . . .
>
> Ephesians 1:7 Phillips

We are grateful that even our blunders may prove useful for Your purposes, Lord.

August 20

The angel announced that Jesus would save His people from their sins (*see* Matthew 1:21). Sometimes we do not grasp that truth and even after we have accepted Jesus as our Saviour we worry about a sin in the past which still burdens us. It is as if we write after the promise of the angel, "except this sin which I have committed." I am sure it is the devil, the accuser of the brethren, who tells us this lie. Listen to the Holy Spirit, not to the liar.

> For our sake he made him to be sin who knew no sin, so that in him we might become the righteousness of God.
>
> 2 Corinthians 5:21 RSV

Lord, I rejoice in You. Forgive my confusion and cleanse my heart and thoughts from all that is wrong.

August 21

Unhappiness in the Christian life is very often due to our failure to realize the greatness of the Gospel. The Gospel is not something partial. It takes in the whole life, the whole of history, the whole world. It tells about the Creation and the final judgment and everything in between. It is a complete, whole view of life. It covers every eventuality in our experience. The Gospel is meant to control and govern everything in our lives. We must dwell more on our riches.

> Let the word of Christ dwell in you richly. . . .
> Colossians 3:16 KJV

How great thou art! Thank You, Lord Jesus, that You came to make us rich King's children instead of poor beggars.

August 22

The moment we become Christians we become the special objects of Satan's attention. He often uses the tool of ridicule to discourage us from doing the work of God. It is his purpose to ruin and destroy the work of the Gospel.

> When Sanballat heard that we were building the wall, he was angry and greatly enraged, and he ridiculed the Jews.
> Nehemiah 4:1 RSV

Lord, Thank You for Your dynamic promises such as "Who is it that overcomes the world but he who believes that Jesus is the Son of God?" Keep us close to Your heart so that we see things, as it were, from Your point of view.

August 23

Do you believe that the Son of God came from heaven and lived and did all He did on earth, that He died on the cross and rose again, that He ascended into heaven and sent the Holy Spirit, in

order to leave us in a state of confusion? Certainly
not; it is impossible.

> This is eternal life, that they know You the only
> true God, and Jesus Christ whom You have sent.
> See John 17:3 RSV

> Holy Spirit, Truth divine,
> Dawn upon this soul of mine.
> Word of God and inward Light,
> Wake my spirit, clear my sight.
> Samuel Longfellow

August 24

The trouble with a man who lacks a clear understanding of justification by faith is that he is still trying to put himself right. It is impossible to pull yourself up by the scruff of your neck. If you do not see
the reality of justification clearly, just talk to the
Lord about it. He is willing to give you full satisfaction.

> God is able to provide you with every blessing in
> abundance, so that you may always have enough
> of everything and may provide in abundance for
> every good work.
> 2 Corinthians 9:8 RSV

Lord Jesus, open my eyes that I may see the many
blessings of eternity which we may enjoy here and
now.

August 25

Do not hastily ascribe all things to God. Do not
easily suppose dreams, voices, impressions, visions,
and revelations to be from God. They may be from
Him, or from nature, or from the devil.

Beloved, do not believe every spirit, but test the spirits to see whether they are of God. . . .
1 John 4:1 RSV

Thank You, Holy Spirit, that You give us the gift of the discernment of the spirits. Keep our vision clear.

August 26

Look unto Jesus. I looked on Jesus and the dove of peace entered my heart. I looked at the dove of peace; and lo . . . off he went.

Once it was the blessing, now it is the Lord.
Once it was the feeling, now it is the Word.
Once the gift I wanted, now the Giver owns.
Once I sought for healing,
    Now Himself alone.

Every good gift and every perfect gift is from above.
James 1:17 KJV

Lord, thank You for all You have given me, but thank You most of all for who You are.

August 27

People know very well that there is no security in today's world. Their knowledge should be counted as a blessing, for it makes them open to the Word of God.

Heaven and earth will pass away, but my words will not pass away.
Matthew 24:35 RSV

When people are insecure, they need help. Lord Jesus, in You we have the help they need. Use us to help all who will listen.

August 28

Many Christians do not realize the work that Jesus is doing today. They forget that He serves as our advocate with His Father, cleansing us of our sins as soon as we confess them.

And if any man sin, we have an advocate with the Father, Jesus Christ the righteous.

1 John 2:1 KJV

Thank You, Jesus, for Your love and that You are there, constantly interceding for us!

August 29

I was number 66,730 in the concentration camp. One day I was called out at roll call and placed as number one in the row. Why did they call me? Could it be that I was to die that day?

Next to me was a Dutch girl. I stood there with her for a long time and I thought, "This is perhaps the last person to whom I can bring the Gospel, for in a short while they will kill me." We had a long talk, and I showed her the whole way of salvation.

Making the most of the time, because the days are evil.

Ephesians 5:16 RSV

Make and keep us faithful to Your work, Lord, no matter what our circumstances are.

August 30

I asked the Dutch girl who stood beside me on roll call, "Do you read the Bible?"

"No, never," she replied.

"Do you know the Lord Jesus?"

"Who is He?"

I told her about Jesus and how He died on the cross for the whole world. I asked her, "Do you ever realize that you need a Saviour? Are you what the Bible calls a sinner?"

"I know I am a sinner," she answered.

"If you have to die here, will you be ready?"

"No."

"Jesus is the answer. He died for the sins of the whole world, and also for your sins."

My sin—oh, the bliss of this glorious thought!—
My sin—not in part, but the whole—
Is nailed to His cross and I bear it no more.
Praise the Lord, praise the Lord, O my soul.

H. G. Spafford

If we confess our sins, he is faithful and just to forgive our sins. . . .

1 John 1:9 KJV

Lord, this is more than I can take in. What a wonderful Saviour You are!

August 31

I continued my talk with the girl I met at roll call.

"Do you know that when you ask Jesus to come into your life and heart, He gives you peace? In perhaps an hour they will kill me, but I am not afraid. I know I belong to Jesus and will go to heaven."

"I would like to know Him," she said.

"Then speak to Him in your heart. He will hear you."

I am the resurrection and the life; he who believes in me, though he die, yet shall he live, and whoever lives and believes in me shall never die. Do you believe this?

John 11:25, 26 RSV

Lord, thank You that You never send away anybody who comes to You.

SEPTEMBER

September 1

On the day which I thought was my last day, the Dutch girl who stood beside me asked me, "How do you know all this that you have told me about Jesus?"

"I know it from the Bible," I answered.

The girl accepted the Lord Jesus as we stood together that morning. I thought she was the last one I would bring to the Lord, but that morning I was set free, not killed.

> . . . lo, I am with you always, even unto the close of the age.
>
> See Matthew 28:20 RSV

Lord, we do not know what this life has in store for us, but be it good or bad, we are willing to be used by You. Use us until that moment comes when we go from service good to service best—when You begin to use us in glory.

September 2

When I am talking to a new child of God, I avoid telling him what he should or should not do in his life. These decisions are better left to the Holy Spirit. It is my job to bring people to Jesus, not to a particular doctrine.

> When the Spirit of truth comes, he will guide you into all the truth.
>
> John 16:13 RSV

Thank You, Lord, that when we bring someone to You, we know that You will take over his guidance for us.

September 3

The glory of friendship is not the outstretched hand, or the kindly smile, or the joy of companionship. It is the spiritual inspiration that comes to one when he discovers that someone else believes in him and is willing to trust him with his friendship.

> No longer do I call you servants, for the servant does not know what his master is doing; but I have called you friends, for all that I have heard from my Father I have made known to you.
>
> John 15:15 RSV

Lord, thank You for the trust You give us when You call us friends. Use us to show others the beauty of friendship for Your sake.

September 4

Either God's Word keeps you from sin, or sin keeps you from God's Word. When a man is truly in Christ, he is saved. All the devil can do is worry him. Say farewell once and forever to your past. It is blotted out in Christ.

> Restore to me the joy of thy salvation. . . .
>
> Psalms 51:12 RSV

Lord Jesus, the devil may worry us, but we are safe in Your keeping. Thank You!

September 5

Don't worry about anything. Tell God every detail of your needs, in earnest and thankful prayer, and receive the peace of God which transcends all human understanding.

> I have said this to you, that in me you may have peace.
>
> John 16:33 RSV

Lord, what a joy that we may come to You with all our troubles. We cannot find peace by ourselves. Thank You that You are willing to listen and that Your telephone line is never "busy."

September 6

The Bible is a book which has been written in order that God's people may see God's way through life. It is an extremely practical book.

Elijah had an attack of spiritual depression after his heroic effort on Mount Carmel (*see* 1 Kings 18, 19). He felt sorry for himself. What he really needed was sleep and food. God have him both.

> And let us not grow weary in well-doing, for in due season we shall reap, if we do not lose heart.
>
> Galatians 6:9 RSV

Lord, You know how tired I am. Will You give me a good night's rest and help me to discipline my diet? Show me if I have done my work in my own strength instead of working in the power of the Holy Spirit.

September 7

We must bear the suffering of other Christians. We must not close our ears and eyes when so many Christians are persecuted. At present, about 60 percent of the Body of Christ are suffering tribulation. Our prayers for them are important and we can know by faith that God can lift their burdens from them through our intercession.

> Bear one another's burdens, and so fulfil the law of Christ.
>
> Galatians 6:2 RSV

Lord, keep us aware of the possibility of suffering before You come again. Take away our fear and make us willing.

September 8

From generation to generation, from small beginnings and little lessons, He has a purpose for those who know and trust Him.

> For who hath despised the day of small things?
>
> Zechariah 4:10 KJV

Lord, I know that even my most insignificant action is part of Your plan after You laid Your hand on my life and I gave my life to You.

September 9

Sometimes I pray with an open Bible and say, "Father, You have promised us this, now I trust that You will do it." I know God likes that for He has meant every promise and He is pleased when we believe His promises.

> And this is the confidence which we have in him, that if we ask anything according to his will he hears us.
>
> 1 John 5:14 RSV

When we ask You to act on Your promises, Father, we are as children asking our parents for food and shelter. We know You will provide for us, for You love us. But we also know that You, as a good parent, do what You see as best for us.

September 10

Do you feel insecure when you talk to learned people about Jesus? They can ask such difficult questions! It is not your job to be wise. God has all the answers, not man. Be content to be an open channel for the Spirit of God. Be obedient and He will give you what you need to be victorious.

> When I came to you, brethren, I did not come proclaiming to you the testimony of God in lofty words or wisdom . . . and my speech and my message were not in plausible words of wisdom, but in demonstration of the Spirit and of power.
>
> 1 Corinthians 2:1, 4 RSV

Lord, thank You that You gave us the Gospel, that the Gospel is for everyone, and that it has the answers for their questions and an abundance for their salvation. Lord, use us to share our riches with them; give us the fullness of Your Holy Spirit.

September 11

God's children have power over Satan through the name of Jesus. As one lone policeman has the power to stop hundreds of vehicles, so one lone believer has the authority to stop Satan and his demons.

> Lord, even the demons are subject to us in your name!
>
> Luke 10:17 RSV

Thank You, Lord, that You make such power and strength available to us.

September 12

"Be filled with the Holy Spirit," is a commandment of the Lord. The enemy is afraid of Spirit-filled people who have the gifts which you read about in 1 Corinthians 12 and 14. He has had great success in making the matters dealt with in these chapters material for quarreling amongst Christians. Don't argue—but obey, and never forget 1 Corinthians 13, for if you have all the gifts and no love—you have nothing.

If I were to speak with the combined eloquence of men and angels I should stir men like a fanfare of trumpets, but unless I had love, I should do nothing more. If I had the gift of foretelling the future and had in my mind not only all human knowledge but the secrets of God, and if, in addition, I had that absolute faith which can move mountains, but had no love, I tell you I should amount to nothing at all.

1 Corinthians 13:1, 2 Phillips

Lord, I need the riches of Your gifts in the serious spiritual battle of this time. Thank You that I am living after Pentecost. Hallelujah!

September 13

The Holy Spirit testifies of Jesus. So when you are filled with the Holy Spirit you speak about our Lord and really live to His honor.

When the Spirit of truth comes, he will guide you into all the truth; for he will not speak on his own authority, but whatever he hears he will speak, and he will declare to you the things that are to come. He will glorify me, for he will take what is mine and declare it to you.

John 16:13, 14 RSV

Thank You, Lord Jesus, that You are willing to fill us again and again with the Holy Spirit and that the fruit and the gifts are available to us. How we need them and how the world around us needs us.

September 14

I possess no special gift that allows me to cast out demons, but there have been times when I felt I had to do it in obedience. I am only one branch of the vine; the blessings may flow through me, but it is God's power that prevails.

In my name they will cast out demons. . . .
Mark 16:17 RSV

All our success is part of Your victory; we claim nothing but Your power, Lord. Show us clearly what Your will is so that we do what we must do.

September 15

It is one thing to cast out demons and another to keep them out. To remain free, a person must stay vigilant in prayer and faithfully build up his spiritual resources. He must resist with determination every effort of Satan to regain entry into his life.

For this very reason make every effort to supplement your faith with virtue, and virtue with knowledge, and knowledge with self-control, and self-control with steadfastness, and steadfastness with godliness, and godliness with brotherly affection, and brotherly affection with love. For if these things are yours and abound, they keep you from being ineffective or unfruitful in the knowledge of our Lord Jesus Christ.
2 Peter 1:5-8 RSV

Thank You, Lord, that You make us more than conquerors in the battle against dark powers.

September 16

We need not fear demons, although they often try to bring fear into our hearts. Never forget that those who are with us are stronger than those who are against us. The weapons of our spiritual warfare are the power of the blood of Jesus and the use of His wonderful name.

> Submit yourselves therefore to God. Resist the devil and he will flee from you.
>
> James 4:7 RSV

Thank You, Lord, that You have given us a divine artillery which silences the enemy and inflicts upon him the damage he would inflict upon us.

September 17

God's Word is ours to accept and rejoice over. Never let your intellect lead you into useless bickering over interpretation. If you are presented with a tasty delicacy, do you stop to analyze it, or do you eat and enjoy it? God's Word is to be savored, not debated.

> And have tasted the goodness of the word of God and the powers of the age to come.
>
> Hebrews 6:5 RSV

Lord Jesus, guide our thinking and speaking. Teach us how to enjoy the promises of God's Word. Make us realize how rich we are through Your grace and love.

September 18

God has sent the Spirit of His Son into our hearts. Do we realize that as Christians we have within us the selfsame Holy Spirit that was in the Lord

Jesus when He was here on earth? The Spirit that enabled Him will enable us.

> Do you not know that your body is a temple of the Holy Spirit within you, which you have from God? You are not your own.
>
> 1 Corinthians 6:19 RSV

Lord, I am longing to be filled and to remain filled with the Holy Spirit. Show me if there is any compromise within me, a "yes, but" or a fear. Forgive and cleanse me, Lord.

September 19

A hospital visitor saw a nurse tending to the sores of a leprosy patient. "I would not do that for a million dollars," he said.

The nurse answered, "Neither would I. But I do it for Jesus for nothing."

> As you did it to one of the least of these my brethren, you did it to me.
>
> Matthew 25:40 RSV

Lord, what You have done for me! What am I doing for You?

September 20

A woman facing a dangerous foreign-mission assignment, when asked if she was afraid to go, replied, "I am afraid of only one thing—that I should become a grain of wheat not willing to die."

> Unless a grain of wheat falls into the earth and dies, it remains alone; but if it dies, it bears much fruit.
>
> John 12:24 RSV

Thank You, Lord, that when I lose my life for Your sake I find it.

September 21

I stood in the Moscow customs office, my suitcase full of Russian Bibles I was smuggling into the country. I saw how the officers ransacked every suitcase, and I was afraid.

I said, "Lord, You have said in the Bible that You watch over Your Word to perform it. The Bibles in my suitcase are Your Word, Lord. Watch over the Bibles."

At that moment I saw light beings around my suitcase. They must have been angels. It is the only time I have seen angels. I can't describe them, for the moment I saw them, they disappeared. But so did my fears!

> Are (angels) not all ministering spirits sent forth to serve, for the sake of those who are to obtain salvation?
>
> Hebrews 1:14 RSV

Thank You, Lord, that those who are with us are more in number and stronger than those who are against us. Hallelujah!

September 22

When I was there in Moscow, my suitcase was the last to receive the attention of the Russian customs officer. "Is that your suitcase, lady?" he asked.

"Yes."

"It is a heavy one!"

"Yes."

He looked around. "Wait. I am done with my work. I can help you carry it to the Intourist car." He picked up the heavy suitcase and carried it to the car for me, never looking inside. How I rejoiced!

... he has said, "I will never fail you nor forsake you." Hence we can confidently say, "The Lord is my helper, I will not be afraid; what can man do to me?"

Hebrews 13:5, 6 RSV

Lord, give me the strength and wisdom to refuse to allow myself to be controlled by a difficult situation. I know that even the hairs of my head are numbered.

September 23

When I worked behind the Iron Curtain it was often dangerous. Life seemed so hard and there were so many sorrows in and around me. Do you know how it feels when dangers are threatening and you are conscious of being weak while the dangers are so strong? I know, and you can know that you are never alone—no, never. Jesus was with me and is with me. Jesus is with you. You are not away from His constant care for one moment.

> Fear not, for I have redeemed you;
> I have called you by name, you are mine.
> When you pass through the waters I will be with you; and through the rivers, they shall not overwhelm you; when you walk through fire you shall not be burned, and the flame shall not consume you.

Isaiah 43:1, 2 RSV

Lord, sorrows and dangers can press upon us. You alone keep us secure. Thank You, Lord, that we stand on victory ground with our weak hands in Your strong hand. Hallelujah!

September 24

Four marks of true repentance are: acknowledgement of wrong, willingness to confess it, willingness to abandon it, and willingness to make restitution.

> According to his promise we wait for new heavens
> and a new earth in which righteousness dwells.
> Therefore, beloved, since you wait for these, be
> zealous to be found by him without spot or blemish,
> and at peace.
>
> 2 Peter 3:13, 14 RSV

Lord, I am willing. Guide me with Your Holy Spirit
to see my sins, to repent, to turn away from my
sin, to confess, and to make it right with people
against whom I have sinned and who have suffered
by my wrong motives and wrong deeds.

September 25

Faith is a

*F*antastic

*A*dventure

*I*n

*T*rusting

*H*im

> Commit your way to the Lord;
> trust in him, and he will act.
>
> Psalms 37:5 RSV

Lord, we may do wondrous things through trusting
in You. Our lives become one continuous adventure,
and we know that the safest place in the world is
the center of Your will.

September 26

Sometimes I am a thermometer—with all the
needs around me, I go down. But we must be thermo-
stats, not thermometers. A thermostat feels cold-
ness and immediately restores the missing heat by

bringing the room in contact with the heater. That
is what we must do.

> Said the Robin to the Sparrow:
> "I should really like to know
> Why these anxious human beings
> Rush about and worry so."

> Said the Sparrow to the Robin,
> "Friend, I think that it must be,
> That they have no heavenly Father,
> Such as cares for you and me."
> Elizabeth Cheney

> . . . Your heavenly Father knoweth that you have
> need of all these things.
> Matthew 6:32 KJV

Father, keep us so close to Your heart that although
we are alert to the needs around us, we will not be depressed by what we see, for You make us able to act
and help.

September 27

Faith is the hand of a beggar reaching out to accept
the gifts of the King. Eternal life is a free gift. It is
given through grace; it is not something earned or de-
served.

> For by grace you have been saved through faith;
> and this is not your own doing, it is the gift of God.
> Ephesians 2:8 RSV

Father, we know we could never earn eternal life.
The fact that You have given it to us freely makes
it even more precious to us.

September 28

Although we continue to sin, and sometimes find it hard to live the victorious life, we must not dwell on our sins, or the devil will lead us into defeatism.

I find it to be a law that when I want to do right, evil lies close at hand.

Romans 7:21 RSV

Take heart, my son; your sins are forgiven.

Matthew 9:2 RSV

Father, the devil sounds so truthful when he tells us how bad we are! On days when his voice is strong, whisper in my hear, "You are forgiven."

September 29

The Bible says God has laid the burden of the sins of the whole world on Jesus. Believe in the Lord Jesus Christ and you will lose your burden.

I have come into the world as light, so that no one who believes in me need remain in the dark.

John 12:46 Phillips

Lord Jesus, thank You that You came into the world in obedience to Your Father. Thank You that You finished at the cross all that had to be done for the salvation of my soul, the cleansing of my heart, and the filling of Your love in my body, soul, and mind.

September 30

"Blessed are those who mourn, for they shall be comforted," said Jesus in Matthew 5:4. How can sorrow do you harm if it is God's way of blessing you? Paul was so grief stricken that he cried out:

Oh, what a terrible predicament I'm in! Who will free me from my slavery to this deadly lower nature? Thank God! It has been done by Jesus Christ our Lord. He has set me free.

Romans 7:24, 25 LB

Lord Jesus, thank You that there is an ocean of love and comfort for me.

OCTOBER

October 1

Blessed are the meek, for they shall inherit the earth. Meekness implies a teachable spirit. The world thinks in terms of strength and power, of ability, self-assurance, and possession. A Christian is different from the world. He belongs to an entirely different Kingdom. Martyrs were meek but they were never weak.

> Take my yoke upon you, and learn of me; for I am meek and lowly in heart: and ye shall find rest unto your souls.
> Matthew 11:29 KJV

Holy Spirit, make me meek so that I can be used as Your tool through Your fruit and Your gifts.

October 2

God's ceiling is unlimited. It requires only need and welcome on our part; the windows of heaven are wide open.

> When all things seem against us—to drive us to despair,
> We know one gate is open—one ear will hear our prayer.
> . . . with God all things are possible.
> Matthew 19:26 KJV

Lord, we know You have the victory in hand. We know everything is possible for You.

October 3

We must never allow ourselves to be agitated and disturbed whatever the circumstances. To do so implies a lack of faith and trust and confidence in our blessed Lord. God gives the gift of faith and then the faith is tried.

> In this you rejoice, though now for a little while you may have to suffer various trials, so that the genuineness of your faith, more precious than gold which though perishable is tested by fire, may redound to praise and glory and honor at the revelation of Jesus Christ.
>
> 1 Peter 1:6, 7 RSV

Thank You, Lord, that You provide and repair our faith whenever it is necessary. Together with You, Lord Jesus, we are victorious.

October 4

The greatest place to bring the Gospel is to your own family. But until the family *sees* what you are talking about, they will never hear your words.

> I am my neighbor's Bible,
> He reads me when we meet,
> Today he reads me in the house,
> Tomorrow in the street.
>
> He may be relative or friend,
> Or slight acquaintance be,
> He may not even know my name,
> Yet he is reading me.
>
> . . . and You shall be witnesses unto me. . . .
>
> Acts 1:8 KJV

Lord, make me a testimony to my family and my neighbors. Take my life as Your channel. Help me to live a life that glorifies You in everything.

October 5

When we were teenagers, each of us children had a Bible in a different language. Mine was in English, Betsie's was in Hebrew, Nollie's in French, and Willem's in Greek. We would compare the Bible verses and that way learn two things at once. These activities in our youth proved to be important in our later lives.

Our training is so complex. Who can say what forms a child into a certain kind of man? Our comfort is that the Lord knows the full story of our lives and will see to the training.

Go into all the world and preach the gospel to the whole creation.

Mark 16:15 RSV

Lord, what a blessing that You understand all the languages of the world and that You gave us Christians the commission to bring the Gospel over the whole earth.

October 6

If you truly love your fellow man, you must warn him of the danger of losing eternal life. Tell everyone you can reach the glorious story of Jesus, that they may be saved in time. The world is full of people who need salvation. It is our job to find them and deliver the message.

There is salvation in no one else, for there is no other name under heaven given among men by which we must be saved.

Acts 4:12 RSV

Holy Spirit, help us not to lose one opportunity.

October 7

I have a book in my hand. The book can be on the table or on the chair, but it must lie somewhere. So it is with our past. Do you bear your past and the sins of your past yourself?

> ... the Lord (God) has laid on him (Jesus) the iniquity of us all.
>
> Isaiah 53:6 RSV

My past is too heavy for me to bear, Lord. It makes me weak and ineffectual. Thank You for taking the burden from me.

October 8

The reality which we see by faith is more important than the results of all our logical thinking.

> We walk by faith, not by sight.
>
> 2 Corinthians 5:7 RSV

Lord, when there is no vision, people perish. Make and keep our faith strong and powerful through Your Holy Spirit so that we see Your pattern.

October 9

There are great lessons to learn concerning faith and the nature or character of faith when you read in the Bible about the disciples. I am grateful for the record of every mistake they ever made and for every blunder they committed. I see myself in them. The Bible speaks the truth and shows and pictures every human frailty.

> And he said to them, "Why are you afraid, O men of little faith?" Then he rose and rebuked the winds and the sea; and there was a great calm.
>
> Matthew 8:26 RSV

Lord, thank You that You do not ask a great faith, but faith in a great God.

October 10

"Thank you for your message, Corrie."

"What was my message?"

"You said that we must believe in God."

"The devil also believes in God, and he trembles! I told you something else. Nobody comes to God without Jesus. It is Him we must accept. We must surrender to Him who bought us with His blood—a very high price. We must give Him His money's worth."

> You were ransomed . . . not with perishable things such as silver or gold, but with the precious blood of Christ. . . .
>
> 1 Peter 1:18, 19 RSV

Lord Jesus, You are the life of my life, the death of my death. How You suffered in body, soul, and mind when You died on the cross for me. Thank You, oh, how I thank You!

October 11

God's all-sufficiency is a major. Your inability is a minor. Major in majors, not in minors. Your ability is not involved. His all-sufficiency and your inability must meet.

> I can do all things in him who strengthens me.
>
> Philippians 4:13 RSV

Thank You, Lord, that Your Holy Spirit enables me to major in Your divine power.

October 12

A prisoner told me, "I decided to follow Jesus, but politics, my car, power, and position came between God and me. This is judgment from God, that I am here."

> The shelf behind the door,
> Tear it down, throw it out,
> Don't use it anymore.
> For Jesus wants your dwelling,
> From the ceiling to the floor.
> He even wants that little shelf
> You keep behind the door.

And he left all, rose up, and followed him
Luke 5:28 KJV

Lord, in Your love You want me 100 percent. I humble myself. Take me, Lord, from head to foot.

October 13

I once visited a weaver's school, where the students were making beautiful patterns. I asked, "When you make a mistake, must you cut it out and start from the beginning?"

A student said, "No. Our teacher is such a great artist that when we make a mistake, he uses it to improve the beauty of the pattern."

That is what the Lord does with our mistakes. He is the greatest artist but we must surrender. Surrender your blunders to the Lord. He can use them to make the pattern of your life more beautiful.

> Faith came singing into my room,
> And other guests took flight.
> Grief, anxiety, fear and gloom,
> Sped out into the night.

I wondered that such peace could be,
But Faith said gently, "Don't you see,
That they can never live with me?"
Elizabeth Cheney

. . . thy faith has made thee whole.
Matthew 9:22 KJV

Lord, we can be so depressed when we blunder. It is wonderful to know that our mistakes can be useful to You, because You are our Master Artist.

October 14

The growth of the Christian life does not stop at the first surrender, any more than marriage stops at the wedding ceremony. The Lord is the potter. We are the clay.

. . . Behold, as the clay is in the potter's hand, so are ye in mine hand, O house of Israel.
Isaiah 18:6 KJV

Have Thine own way, Lord, Have Thine own way!
Thou art the Potter, I am the clay.
Mold me and make me, After Thy will,
While I am waiting, Yielded and still.
Adelaide A. Pollard

October 15

If you lose yourself for Jesus' sake, you cannot hold out on anything. No "excepts" are accepted!

I said, "Let me walk in the fields."
He said, "No, walk in the town."
I said, "There are no flowers there."
He said, "No flowers, but a crown."
George MacDonald

For where your treasure is, there will your heart be also.

Matthew 6:21 KJV

Lord Jesus, forgive my "excepts." I surrender anew and now totally. My mind and body may say I cannot, but with the help of the Holy Spirit, I can.

October 16

If you are angry, don't sin by nursing your grudge. Don't let the sun go down while you are still angry. Get it over quickly, for when you are angry you give a mighty foothold to the devil. It is such a blessing that we can bring our anger immediately to the Lord. He is able and willing to fill our hearts with His love.

> Be angry but do not sin; do not let the sun go down on your anger.

Ephesians 4:26 RSV

Lord, thank You that sin no longer has victory over us because of Your victory on the cross and Your Resurrection.

October 17

There is no neutrality on the front line of the battle between light and darkness. Walk only in the light. When a Christian shuns fellowship with other Christians, the devil smiles. When he stops reading the Bible, the devil laughs. When he stops praying, the devil shouts for joy.

> If thou but suffer God to guide thee,
> And hope in Him through all thy ways,
> He'll give thee strength, whate'er betide thee,
> And bear thee thro' the evil days;

Who trusts in God's unchanging love
Builds on the rock that naught can move.

George Neumark

. . . We ought to obey God rather than men.

Acts 5:29 KJV

Forgive me, Lord, that I tried the detour of a compromise. Have Your own way, Lord. Hold over my being absolute sway.

October 18

Some people trust the Lord for eternal salvation but not for the cares of everyday life. Feed your faith—that starves your doubt to death.

I look to Thee in every need,
And never look in vain;
I feel Thy strong and tender love,
And all is well again:
The thought of Thee is mightier far,
Than sin and pain and sorrow are.

Samuel Longfellow

Ask, and it shall be given you. . . .

Matthew 7:7 KJV

Father, keep doubts from our minds. Build our faith until we can follow You without fear and care.

October 19

Cast your burden on the Lord. Don't try to solve the world's problems with your mind. You cannot unscramble scrambled eggs.

I want you to be free from anxieties.

1 Corinthians 7:32 RSV

The world is Your concern, Father. Thank You that You are willing to use even me for Your purposes.

October 20

Rebellion against the Holy Spirit makes a vacuum that the devil likes to fill.

> Obey my voice, and I will be your God, and you shall be my people; and walk in all the way that I command you, that it may be well with you.
> Jeremiah 7:23 RSV

Make me content to work where I have been called, Father.

October 21

God's resources are not limited to our natural abilities. We cannot use the excuse that we are not qualified. Remember the parable of the talents.

> It is the man who shares my life and whose life I share who proves fruitful. For apart from me you can do nothing at all.
> John 15:5 Phillips

Thank You, Lord, for the unlimited power with which You are at work in us who believe.

October 22

The moment we seek of ourselves to please God, we are placing ourselves under the law, a realm where grace does not operate. Grace implies that God does something for us. Law implies that we do something for God. Deliverance from the law does not mean that we are free from doing the will of God, but that another, the Lord Himself, does it in us and through us.

> For sin will have no dominion over you, since you are not under law but under grace.
> Romans 6:14 RSV

Lord, increase my capacity to receive Your grace. I am willing to humble myself.

October 23

The enemy will try to separate us from God, to destroy our faith, and make us rebel.

> Be sober, be watchful. Your adversary the devil prowls around like a roaring lion, seeking some one to devour. Resist him, firm in your faith, knowing that the same experience of suffering is required of your brotherhood throughout the world.
>
> 1 Peter 5:8, 9 RSV

We are willing to suffer for You, Lord. Strengthen our faith so that Satan will be foiled in his attempts to come between You and us.

October 24

It is only on earth that there are those who do not believe in God. Even though the powers of evil lead men astray and keep them in darkness and unbelief, they themselves believe in God and tremble, for they know that on the Lord's day, judgment awaits them.

> And the devil . . . was cast into the lake of fire and brimstone, where the beast and the false prophet are. . . .
>
> Revelation 20:10 KJV

Lord, help us to remember our final triumph with You when we are tormented by the evil one.

October 25

We must watch out for occult sins. Even when you say you do not believe that fortune-teller, and are going just for fun, it is dangerous, and will come between you and the Lord.

> There shall not be found among you any one that maketh his son or his daughter to pass through the fire, or that useth divination, or an observer of times, or an enchanter, or a witch, Or a charmer, or a consulter with familiar spirits, or a wizard, or a necromancer. For all that do these things are an abomination unto the Lord.
>
> Deuteronomy 18:10-12 KJV

Thank You, Lord Jesus, that if we have done these abominations and confess our sins, You are faithful and just to forgive us and to liberate us totally. You will cleanse our bodies, souls, and minds with Your blood. Hallelujah!

October 26

Divination is fortune-telling. Observers of times are astrologers. An enchanter is a magician. A witch is a sorcerer. A charmer is a hypnotist. Consulters with familiar spirits are mediums. A wizard is a clairvoyant. A necromancer is one who consults with the dead.

To have God's guidance, you need to make a clean break from all other forms of guidance. Guidance is something we must ask for and desire. God wants your submission, and will steadily guide you.

> When he, the Spirit of truth, is come, he will guide you into all truth . . . he will shew you things to come.
>
> John 16:13 KJV

Keep us faithful through all temptations, Lord. Show us the truth.

October 27

The world is becoming increasingly uninhabitable, but we have hope for the world's future because of God's promises. Crisis always demands spiritual qualities. None of us can refuse to face the storms. The tree on the mountain takes whatever the weather brings. If it has any choice at all, it is simply in putting down roots as deeply as possible, and getting ready to withstand. Defense is something deep and invisible.

Did we in our own strength confide,
Our striving would be losing,
Were not the right Man on our side,
The Man of God's own choosing.
Dost ask who that may be? Christ Jesus, it is He;
Lord Sabaoth His name. From age to age the
    same,
And He must win the battle.

Martin Luther

Therefore take the whole armor of God, that you may be able to withstand in the evil day, and having done all, to stand.

Ephesians 6:13 RSV

Our roots are in You, Lord. They hold firm in any storm that tears at our bodies, souls, and spirits.

October 28

We do not report to any special place for our training in God's army. We train where we are, using all of our everyday experiences and our contacts with other people. Training in the field is harder than training in the camp, but it makes better soldiers.

Soldier, soldier, fighting in the world's great
strife,
On yourself relying, battling for your life.
Trust yourself no longer,
Trust in Christ, He's stronger!
You can all things, all things, do
Through Christ who strengthens you.

Finally, be strong in the Lord and in the strength
of his might.

Ephesians 6:10 RSV

Lord, I enroll in Your service. Make me willing
to be made willing to do Your will.

October 29

Everyday life is our front line in the war against
the devil. God Himself must decide where each of
us is to fight. We cannot choose the battlefield we
prefer. If you conquered a problem today in the
strength of Jesus Christ, that was a victory. You
are now stronger for the end battle.

And though this world, with devils filled,
Should threaten to undo us,
We will not fear, for God hath willed,
His truth to triumph through us.
The Prince of Darkness grim,
We tremble not for him;
His rage we can endure,
For lo! his doom is sure;
One little word shall fell him.

Martin Luther

But thanks be to God, who gives us the victory
through our Lord Jesus Christ.

1 Corinthians 15:57 RSV

Give us the grace to fight wherever You choose to place us, Lord. Only You can see the battlefield completely; we see only one small part of it.

October 30

The Lord taught me through my prison experiences that for a child of God, a pit can be very deep, but always deeper are the everlasting arms of our Lord.

> But even if you do suffer for righteousness' sake, you will be blessed. Have no fear of them, nor be troubled.
>
> 1 Peter 3:14 RSV

Thank You, Lord, that no matter how deep our distress, Your comfort is always sufficient for our needs. You have promised to be with us until the end of the world.

October 31

When you don't understand something in the Bible, don't throw it away, but hang it on the hook for the time being. I read in Ezekiel 38:4 that the enemy will come on horseback, but today the army does not ride on horses. Then I read in the newspaper that Russia has bought 70 percent of the world's horses for its army! I had put Ezekiel 38 on the hook, but it came off again. Don't throw away what you do not understand.

> God holds the key of all unknown,
> And I am glad.
> If other hands should hold the key,
> Or if He trusted it to me,
> I might be sad.

Trust in him at all times, O people . . . God is a refuge for us.

It is not for us to understand everything. Our duty is simply to obey, trusting in Your guidance and protection, Lord.

NOVEMBER

November 1

I was at the end of my first week in America and practically at the end of my money. The clerk at the YWCA had told me I could not stay there another week. Where should she forward my mail?

"I don't know yet. God has a room for me but He has not told me where yet."

I could see by the look on her face that she was concerned about me. Then she handed me a piece of mail which she had overlooked. The letter was from a woman who heard me speak in New York. She was offering me the use of her son's room.

I gave the amazed clerk my new address after thanking God for His care.

But my God shall supply all your need. . . .
Philippians 4:19 KJV

Thank You, Lord, that we may know that our need is never greater than the Helper.

November 2

Jesus was obedient to the Father. Read His story. When He was twelve years old He obeyed His earthly parents, at the same time knowing that He had to be busy with the things of His heavenly Father. When John the Baptist tried to stop Him from being baptized, He said He wanted to have baptism as a sign of obedience. How glorious it was when the Holy Spirit came down on Him and the Father spoke from heaven: "This is my beloved

Son, with whom I am well pleased" (Matthew 3:17 RSV).

To obey is better than sacrifice. . . .
1 Samuel 15:22 RSV

Holy Spirit, let me know whether there is any disobedience in my life. I want to do what You want.

November 3

Difficulties exist in order to be overcome. Because Jesus made us yokefellows with Him, we are able to be overcomers.

My times are in Thy hand;
Jesus the crucified!
The hand our many sins had pierced,
Is now my guard and guide.

My times are in Thy hand;
I'll always trust in Thee;
Until I've left the weary land,
And all Thy glory see.

William F. Lloyd

Him that overcometh will I make a pillar in the temple of my God. . . .
Revelation 3:12 KJV

Lord Jesus, thank you that through Your strength we can be overcomers.
We will trust our path to You, Lord, sure of Your guidance and support every step of the way.

November 4

When Holland surrendered to Germany, Father and I walked in the street. We felt a great oneness with everybody around us. We were all together in the great suffering, humiliation, and defeat of our nation. Everybody talked with everybody else. I have never before or since experienced such oneness in the nation. It was a great blessing.

We will be that way in the millennium, but the oneness will not be in misery but in our communication with the Lord.

> Behold, the tabernacle of God is with men, and he will dwell with them, and they shall be his people, and God himself shall be with them, and be their God.
>
> Revelation 21:3 KJV

Lord Jesus, when we experience great closeness with our fellow men, that warmth and communication is only a foretaste of what we have waiting in store for us. What a blessing to anticipate. Hallelujah!

November 5

Synchronize your watch with heaven's clock. You can do that by reading the Bible together with the newspaper. Then you will know that we live in the time when we can expect Jesus' coming again to earth very soon.

Listen closely to what the Lord is willing to tell you. The Holy Spirit can make your prayer and conversation with Himself a joyful speaking and listening.

Read important books which will strengthen your faith.

> I am sure that he who began a good work in you will bring it to completion at the day of Jesus Christ.
>
> Philippians 1:6 RSV

Lord Jesus, You are looking forward to the great day of Your coming. I am looking forward, too. Make me ready, Lord. I surrender with joy.

November 6

Do you know that we are living in the last days and that they are the first days of a beautiful future? What are you doing to win souls? What are you doing to make people ready for Jesus' coming again? To bring the Gospel over the whole world is a fundamental part of the life of a Christian.

Occupy till I come.

Luke 19:13 KJV

Show me my program for today, Lord. Give me the guidance and power to make it important in Your eyes.

November 7

"We know that the whole creation has been groaning in travail together until now" (Romans 8:22 RSV).

The restless millions wait
The coming of the Lord to make all things new.
Christ also waits.
But men are slow and few.
Have we done all we could?
Have I? Have you?

Thank You, Lord, that we know from the Bible that the crisis we experience in this time is the suffering You told about when You said that we must look up because our liberation is approaching (*see* Luke 21).

November 8

It *is* possible for you and me to be ready for Jesus' coming. The surrendered self is dynamic since it is the branch that is connected with the Living Vine.

> I am the vine, you are the branches.
>> John 15:5 RSV

Our hope is in the Living Vine through which Your love flows freely, Father.

November 9

"Peace on earth." That statement by the angels will find its perfection when Jesus comes to make all things new. The whole world will be covered with the knowledge of God as the waters cover the bottom of the sea.

> In those days the world will be ruled from Jerusalem. The Lord will settle international disputes; all the nations will convert their weapons of war into implements of peace.
>> Isaiah 2:3, 4 LB

Lord, thank You that You are preparing the world for that great future. Please prepare me, too.

November 10

To receive God's guidance you need to make a clean break from all other forms of guidance. Do not look at the stars, at the palm of your hand, or listen to a fortune-teller. These things are an abomination in God's sight.

> God knows the future.
> God plans the future.
> God has told us the future in His Word.

> You shall be blameless before the Lord your God.
>> Deuteronomy 18:13 RSV

Lord Jesus, forgive me for looking in the wrong direction. Teach me Your way.

November 11

Once I asked a parachutist, "How did you feel when you jumped from an airplane with a parachute on your back for the first time?"

He answered, "There was only one thought: 'It works, it works!' "

What does it mean to go through life with Jesus? I can answer from experience, "It works, it works!"

> ... in all these things we win an overwhelming victory through Him Who has proved His love for us.
>
> Romans 8:37 Phillips

Lord, what joy that we may tell other people that it works. Hallelujah!

November 12

When I was a tramp for the Lord, I was once worried about my work. Where must I go? Will there be a room? Where can I live? Will there be people to take care of meetings? Must I go to that difficult country, Russia? It can be very rough there. I opened the Bible and read Psalm 23. Great joy came into my heart. As a sheep of the Good Shepherd I had nothing to fear.

> The Lord is my shepherd, I shall not want;
> he makes me lie down in green pastures.
>
> Psalms 23:1, 2 RSV

Lord, fill our hearts, our consciousness, and our subconsciousness with Your peace and love. Then we will not fear, even though the earth should be

removed and the mountains thrown into the heart
of the sea (*see* Psalms 46:2). Hallelujah!

November 13

All of us have sinned and come short of the
glory of God. No one can say, "I am good." The
basis of trust is Jesus' finished work—not what I
have done but what *He* has done.

It is finished.

John 19:30 RSV

Lord Jesus, thank You for the rich inheritance You
gave us.

November 14

The suffering of prisoners is so deep. They have
no freedom. The discipline they endure often comes
from cruel guards. They have contact with unhappy
and bad people, often day and night, and these bad
people often cause them to sin. Sometimes they
are heavily burdened because of the suffering they
have brought on their family through their crimes.

. . . I was in prison and you came to me.

Matthew 25:36 RSV

Lord, show me what I can do for prisoners. I am
willing to be used.

November 15

Nothing sets a person so far out of the devil's
reach as humility.

If my people who are called by my name humble
themselves, and pray and seek my face, and turn
from their wicked ways, then I will hear from

heaven, and will forgive their sin and heal their land.

2 Chronicles 7:14 RSV

Lord, I am willing to humble myself.

November 16

When God speaks you always have to give an answer. That answer is either yes or no. To give no answer is the same as to say no.

Are you ready for Jesus Christ or for Antichrist?

It is time to get really serious with God. Give your answer now. After you have done that, have a talk with the Lord and ask Him, "What did that mean for me, Lord, that I said yes/no?"

> And can it be that I should gain
> An interest in the Saviour's blood?
> Died He for me, who caused His pain?
> For me, who Him to death pursued?
> Amazing love! how can it be
> That Thou, my God, shouldst die for me?
>
> Charles Wesley

I call upon thee, for thou wilt answer me, O God. . . .
Psalms 17:6 RSV

Thank You, Lord, that You said yes to me, and that now my answer—yes—is possible.

November 17

Nothing limits the supplies we can obtain from God except our capacity to take. After surrender, the Holy Spirit makes us capable of taking.

> Oh, the love that drew salvation's plan!
> Oh, the grace that bro't it down to man!

Oh, the mighty gulf that God did span,
At Calvary.

William R. Newell

May the God of hope fill you with all joy and peace
in believing. . . .

Romans 15:13 RSV

Thank You, Lord, for Your ocean of love.

November 18

"Your will be done," is not an expression of resignation but of resolution. It is active, not passive. The secret of Jesus' obedience was that He loved God. A child who loves its parents wants to obey them because he or she knows that that gives them joy.

Our Father who art in heaven,
Hallowed be thy name.
Thy kingdom come,
Thy will be done,
On earth as it is in heaven.

Matthew 6:9, 10 RSV

Lord, I surrender my will to You. Where it is difficult for me, I pray that You will make me willing to be made willing to do Your will.

November 19

Read Ephesians 3:14-19. Add the length and breadth and height and depth of the love of God, and the sum cannot be multiplied enough to express His love for me, the least of His children. God sees you and me in the midst of millions. He knows your name and He is close to you. Don't pray, "Come closer to me." A fish does not ask the water to come closer to it and a bird does not ask the air to come closer. They are already as close as they can be, and in the same way God is close to you.

> ... remember, I am with you always, even to the
> end of the world.
>> Matthew 28:20 Phillips

How secure I am in Your constant intensive care. Thank You, Lord.

November 20

The Lord can do more with three blessed quarters than with an unblessed three hundred dollars.

> ... which is more important, the gift, or the altar
> which sanctifies the gift?
>> Matthew 23:19 Phillips

O Lord, teach us to look at all things, including gifts, with Your values in mind, so that we may see the worth of the smallest gift or the danger of the largest.

November 21

Keep looking up and kneeling down. Then you can keep looking down from the position of Jesus' victory over your problems. He is willing to make you more than conqueror.

> Look around and be distressed
> Look within and be depressed
> Look at Jesus and be at rest.

> ... in all these things we are more than con-
> querors through him who loved us.
>> Romans 8:37 RSV

Thank You, Lord Jesus, that we can look at You through faith and that You are the author and finisher of our faith. Hallelujah!

November 22

When are our sins covered by the sacrifice of Christ? When we confess them: "If we confess our sins, he if faithful and just, and will forgive our sins and cleanse us from all unrighteousness" (1 John 1:9 RSV).

But that is not the whole truth—our sins were covered when Jesus Christ died on the cross more than nineteen hundred years ago.

> He who believes in him is not condemned; he who does not believe is condemned already, because he has not believed in the name of the only Son of God.
>
> John 3:18 RSV

The problem is not that we sin but that we reject the remedy. Yes, Lord Jesus, yes! I will not reject Your remedy. I confess my sin and accept Your answer.

November 23

A proper response to the Lord in thanksgiving for our salvation is to spread the Gospel throughout the world.

> . . . you shall be my witnesses in Jerusalem and in all Judea and Samaria and to the end of the earth.
>
> Acts 1:8 RSV

Father, all You ask is that we obey You and do Your work. You give us the equipment—not a spirit of fear but of power, of love, and a sound mind.

November 24

Do you ever have the feeling that you are not good enough to come to the Lord for salvation? Jesus has said, "I came not to call the righteous, but sinners to repentance" (Luke 5:32 KJV). The very thing you are saying in self-condemnation is the very thing that gives you the right to come to Him and to be certain that He will receive you. Christ is the friend of publicans and sinners. He came to die for such people.

> (Jesus Christ) gave himself for us to redeem us from all iniquity and to purify for himself a people of his own who are zealous for good deeds.
>
> Titus 2:14 RSV

Lord Jesus, thank You that I may come to You just as I am.

November 25

Some people sing and pray, "Let Thy congregation escape tribulation," but Jesus said that in the world we will have tribulation.

> Blessed are they which are persecuted for righteousness' sake: for theirs is the kingdom of heaven. ...Rejoice, and be exceeding glad: for great is your reward in heaven.
>
> Matthew 5:10, 12 KJV

Thank You, Lord Jesus, that You have overcome the world. Together with You we are victorious even in tribulation, problems, and trials. We can see our problems and trials as a part of Your embroidery of our life.

November 26

How is the situation of the enemy? The strategy of a defeated enemy is different. When God's people advance, the enemy will crumble. A church is a battering ram, bashing in the gates of hell. The Word of God is our weapon.

> For though we live in the world we are not carrying on a a worldly war, for the weapons of our warfare are not worldly but have divine power to destroy strongholds.
>
> 2 Corinthians 10:3, 4 RSV

Holy Spirit, give us a clear vision of the situation of our enemy, our own army, and ourselves, but most of all of our King of Kings.

November 27

Conditions in our barracks in the concentration camp at Ravensbruck were terrible. When we first arrived I told Betsie I could not bear the lice that lived in our filthy blankets and mattresses. She replied, "You must thank God for everything, even for lice." Betsie was right. Because of the bugs which infested our barrack, the women guards and officers kept their distance, and we were able to hold our Bible studies without fear. God had a use for the vermin, after all! Sometimes what we see as a curse one day becomes a blessing the next day. How much more simple it would be if we would learn to thank God for everything instead of using our own judgment.

> Always and for everything giving thanks in the name of our Lord Jesus Christ to God the Father.
>
> Ephesians 5:20 RSV

Lord, I need a miracle by Your Holy Spirit to thank You for my problem of today. Thank You that You are willing to make me willing.

November 28

Father prayed because he had a good friend with whom to share the problems of the day. He prayed because he had a direct connection with his Maker when he had a concern. He prayed because there was so much for which he was thankful.

> Rejoice in your hope, be patient in tribulation, be constant in prayer.
>
> Romans 12:12 RSV

Our lives are full of reasons for prayer, Father. We know You want us to tell You everything because You care for us deeply. Thank You for Your constant care.

November 29

The testing of your faith today is training for the great end battle. Are you victorious today? Then you are stronger than you were yesterday. An athlete does not complain when the training is hard; he thinks ahead to the coming competition.

> We follow a scarred captain.
> Should not we have scars?
> Under His mighty banner
> We are going to the wars.
> Lest we forget, Lord, when we meet
> Show us Your hands and feet.
>
> Amy Carmichael

> For you know that the testing of your faith produces steadfastness.
>
> James 1:3 RSV

Lord, You are the source of our strength. We will not complain that our training is hard, for so is the battle to come.

November 30

None of us can afford to be anything less than absolutely controlled by the Holy Spirit. Let God have His way with you, because if you do not that unconsecrated thing, that sinful habit in your life will be a foothold for the devil to wreck your witness. Seeing that the devil is working so insidiously in the churches, let us come to God in these last days and tell Him that we want to be altogether His, devoted to Him, led by Him, filled with His Spirit, taught of Him, so that we may be kept from sin and at the same time may be ready for the glorious event when we shall see Jesus face to face.

Brother Langston

May the God of peace make you holy through and through. May you be kept in soul and mind and body in spotless integrity until the coming of our Lord Jesus Christ.

1 Thessalonians 5:23 Phillips

Lord Jesus, thank You that You died for us and live for us to make us able to live for You.

DECEMBER

December 1

The month of December—the month of Christmas. Does that mean for you being extra busy, giving all your spare time to planning presents? The Lord Jesus did not come to make you overly busy. The angels spoke about peace on earth. Claim the promise of James 1:5 for wisdom about how to organize your time and what kind of Christmas presents to give. It is possible that the Lord will give you guidance to give Christian books. A good book given at Christmas will remain a blessing long after the twenty-fifth of December.

> If any of you lacks wisdom, let him ask God, who gives to all men generously and without reproaching, and it will be given him.
>
> James 1:5 RSV

Lord Jesus, I claim the fruit of the Spirit called peace for this Christmas month.

December 2

You need Jesus. "If onlies" can become a barrier to Him. "If only my husband gave me more time and love." "If only my teenagers were more obedient." "If only I had more money." "If only my dad understood me better."

Surrender your "if onlies." They stand in the way. When you do surrender, you belong to the Lord, with all the "if onlies." That is good!

> The Spirit, however, produces in human life fruits such as these: love, joy, peace, patience, kindness, generosity, fidelity, adaptability and self-control. . . .
> Galatians 5:22 Phillips

Lord, teach us to rise above our petty problems, so that we may use all our talents to overcome the greater problems of the world.

December 3

If God has called you, do not spend time looking over your shoulder to see who is following. Sometimes I think that some young men who heard the challenge to surrender their lives and go to the mission field gave the answer, "Lord, take my life, but send my sister."

> All authority in heaven and on earth has been given to me. *Go* therefore and make disciples of all nations. . . .
> Matthew 28:18, 19 RSV, author's italics

> I'll go where You want me to go, dear Lord,
> Over mountain, or plain, or sea;
> I'll say what You want me to say, dear Lord,
> I'll be what You want me to be.
> Mary Brown

December 4

In heaven you will see how the Lord has used that testimony, that word of comfort you gave today. God's Word never returns void.

> When you enter the beautiful city,
> And the saved all around you appear,
> What joy when someone will tell you,
> "It was you who invited me here."

From the fruit of his words a man is satisfied with good, and the work of a man's hand comes back to him.

Proverbs 12:14 RSV

Lord, we like to see results from our labor, but it is not necessary that we do. We trust You to complete the work You are doing in and through us.

December 5

As victory is the result of Christ's life lived out in the believer, it is important to see that victory, not defeat, is God's purpose for His children.

Can anything separate us from the love of Christ? Can trouble, pain or persecution? Can lack of clothes and food, danger to life and limb, the threat of force of arms? . . . No, in all these things we win an overwhelming victory through Him Who has proved his love for us.

Romans 8:35, 37 Phillips

Thank You, Lord Jesus, that our final victory is secure because of Your sacrifice upon the cross, Your rising from the dead, and Your glorification in heaven, where You plead for us.

December 6

A man and his son went over a long, narrow bridge. It was over a broad river, and the boy said, "Daddy, I am afraid. Do you see all that water down there?"

"Give me your hand, boy," the father said. The moment the boy felt his father's hand, he was not scared. In the evening they had to go back again, and this time it was pitch dark.

"Now I am more afraid than this morning!" the

boy cried. The father took the little fellow in his arms. Immediately the boy fell asleep, to awaken the next day in his own bed. That is what death is like for the Christian. He falls asleep and wakes up at Home.

> Afraid of what?
> To feel the Spirit's glad release,
> To pass from pain to perfect peace,
> The strife and strain of life to cease,
> Afraid of that?
>
> Afraid of what?
> Afraid to see the Saviour's face,
> To hear His welcome and to trace,
> The glory gleams of wounds of grace,
> Afraid of that?

O death, where is thy victory? O death, where is thy sting?

1 Corinthians 15:55 RSV

Lord Jesus, thank You that You have conquered death. What a comfort to be safe in Your arms. Thank You that You are always there to take our trembling hands in Your strong hands.

December 7

Life is immortal, love eternal; death is nothing but a horizon, and a horizon is only the limit of our vision.

If a man keep my saying, he shall never see death.

John 9:51

Thank You, Lord, that we possess eternal life here and now. That gives us vision regarding present and future, earth and heaven.

December 8

Everyone needs a place to be. One of the great joys of heaven is that it is a place, a prepared place. I am thankful that there I will have a special house that is reserved just for me.

> In my Father's house are many mansions: if it were not so, I would have told you. I go to prepare a place for you.
>
> John 14:2 KJV

Lord Jesus, thank You for the assurance of a heavenly home. A place to rest, a place to be, is important to our lives, both now and in the future.

December 9

Joseph filled the barns in the time of plenty to be prepared for the time of famine (*see* Genesis 41:29-36). Gather the riches of God's promises which can strengthen you in the time when there will be no freedom. Nobody can take away from you those texts from the Bible which you have learned by heart.

> So that there will be enough to eat when the seven years of famine come.
>
> Genesis 41:36 LB

Lord Jesus, we do not fear the future because we know You who have the future in Your hand. What a joy to know that You are the same yesterday, today, and forever.

December 10

Keep constant guard over your hearts and minds as they rest in Christ Jesus. Worries carry responsibilities that belong to God, not to you. Worry does

not enable us to escape evil; it makes us unfit to
cope with it when it comes. You may see all the
reasons for failure, but God sees all the reasons
for success!

Will your anchor hold in the storms of life,
When the clouds unfold their wings of strife?
When the strong tides lift and the cables strain,
Will your anchor drift or firm remain?

We have an anchor that keeps the soul
Steadfast and sure while the billows roll,
Fastened to the rock which cannot move,
Grounded firm and deep in the Savior's love.

Priscilla Owens

And the peace of God . . . will keep your hearts and
your minds in Christ Jesus.

Philippians 4:7 RSV

Thank You, Lord Jesus, that with You as our anchor,
we need never fear.

December 11

Every Bible student who believes the prophecies
knows that Jesus' coming is very near. The important, urgent thing is that every child of God must
be prepared for that day. That is possible for everybody. Jesus finished all that had to be done for us
on the cross. He died for us and rose again and
is with the Father, where He prays for us. By His
Holy Spirit He is even in us. If you know you are
not ready, confess your sins and claim God's forgiveness for Jesus' sake. Forgive others by the
power of the Holy Spirit in you.

Because . . . you have a hope like this before you, I urge you to make certain that such a Day would find you at peace with God and man, clean and blameless in His sight.

2 Peter 3:14 Phillips

Thank You, Lord Jesus, that You are willing to prepare me to meet You, whenever that will be.

December 12

When God allows extraordinary trials for His people, He prepares extraordinary comforts for them. Tribulation is God's thorny but blessed way to glorious victory.

God has said, "I will never, *never* fail you nor forsake you."

Hebrews 13:5 LB

Thank You, Lord, that we have nothing to fear, for You are with us. Together with You, we are able to bear suffering and trials.

December 13

When I was a child, whenever we had to go to the doctor or dentist, Papa went with us to comfort us. He never said we would not have pain, but that we must be brave and strong. Holding his hand gave us courage.

It is the same with God. He never promised we would not have pain in our lives, but holding His hand gives us courage.

Who comforts us in all our affliction, so that we may be able to comfort those who are in any affliction, with the comfort with which we ourselves are comforted by God.

2 Corinthians 1:4 RSV

Our God and Father, thank You for Your fatherly hand in times of trouble. We need Your comfort so much, and willingly share it with those who suffer along with us.

December 14

Opposition to lives which are yielded to Jesus Christ takes many forms, some dramatic, some subtle. In my life I have experienced opposition in the form of supernatural sounds, superficial attitudes from the self-righteous, and from within myself. I have had doubt in my heart and dryness in my prayer life. I stood on the front line of the battle, but through Jesus it was victory ground.

> What shall we then say to these things? If God be for us, who can be against us?
>
> Romans 8:31 KJV

When we are in fear and despair, help us to remember that You, Jesus, have given us the victory in advance, and we are bound to win the battle we face.

December 15

When I first began to show people the danger of occult sin, fearful thoughts came to me. I would return from a meeting completely exhausted, with my heart beating irregularly. I feared I would die if I continued, so I asked the Lord to release me from the burden. He showed me the following verses:

> Do not be afraid, but speak and do not be silent; for I am with you, and no man shall attack you to harm you. . . .
>
> Acts 18:9, 10 RSV

Lord Jesus, show us when we are keeping silent because of fear. Give us the faith and courage to speak up whenever it is necessary.

December 16

God never inspires doubt and fear, but faith and courage. Peter produced his own doubts by looking at the waves.

I sought the Lord, and he answered me,
and delivered me from all my fears.
Psalms 34:4 RSV

Lord, our fears are the result of not trusting fully in You. Make us see the foolishness of fearing. Turn our eyes in the right direction unto You, Lord, and away from the waves.

December 17

Faith brings us on highways that make our reasoning dizzy.

His unchanging plan has always been to adopt us into his own family by sending Jesus Christ to die for us. And he did this because he wanted to! Now all praise to God for his wonderful kindness to us and his favor that he has poured out upon us, because we belong to his dearly loved Son.
Ephesians 1:5, 6 LB

O Lord, how rich I am. Forgive me for worrying so much, and cleanse me.

December 18

I was often afraid as a small child. I begged my sister, Nollie, to let me hold her hand as we slept. Then, when I was five, the Lord Jesus became a great reality to me. I asked Him to come live in my heart, and a feeling of peace and security took the place of the fear I had felt before. From then on I could go to sleep at night and not be afraid.

> I sought the Lord, and he answered me,
> and delivered me from all my fears.
>
> Psalms 34:4 RSV

Deep inside, hidden from the world, we are often fearful little children, Lord. We awake in the night, afraid until You whisper, "Hush, I am here."

December 19

We will see more and more that we are chosen not because of our ability but because of the Lord's power, which will be demonstrated in our not being able.

> When they deliver you up, do not be anxious how you are to speak or what you are to say; for what you are to say will be given to you in that hour.
>
> Matthew 10:19 RSV

Lord, what a joy, what an honor that You will use me, even me, as a light in this dark world.

December 20

Many Christians think that when they are born again that is the end. I once spoke about the strong challenge of the Beatitudes and how we can live a victorious life if we hunger and thirst after righteousness. Victory means a surrender of self from head to foot, again and again. I asked a dear Christian woman what her answer was. She said, "I surrendered twelve years ago when I accepted

Jesus as my Saviour." But the Bible says, "Be filled with the Holy Spirit." A newborn baby has to grow.

I have known the Lord Jesus for eighty years. As I studied the Bible in writing these messages, I had to surrender and be cleansed and filled again and again.

> . . . I came that they may have life, and have it abundantly.
>
> John 10:10 RSV

We praise You, Lord Jesus, that You not only gave us life when we were born again but Your Word and Your Holy Spirit also make us grow into the life abundant.

December 21

Paul said in Colossians 1:24 that he was privileged to make up in his own body what remains of the suffering of Christ. What if you and I as Christians are having the same privilege without knowing it? Ask the Lord to forgive you that you ever allowed yourself to be weary. That will give you new hope, new strength, and new power.

> Well done, good and faithful servant . . . enter into the joy of your master.
>
> Matthew 25:23 RSV

Lord Jesus, I know that I am victorious when I am Your yokefellow.

December 22

> I used to ask God to help me. Then I asked if I might help him. I ended up by asking God to do his work through me.
>
> Hudson Taylor

Unless the Lord builds the house,
those who build it labor in vain.

Psalms 127:1 RSV

Thank You, Lord, that You do the job.

December 23

"Blessed are the poor in spirit, for theirs is the kingdom of heaven" (Matthew 5:3 RSV). We cannot be filled until we are empty. We have to be poor in spirit of ourselves in order to be filled with the Holy Spirit. "In my hand no price I bring; Simply to Thy cross I cling. . . ."

> For thus says the high and lofty One who inhabits eternity, whose name is Holy: "I dwell in the high and holy place, and also with him who is of a contrite and humble spirit, to revive the spirit of the humble, and to revive the heart of the contrite."

Isaiah 57:15 RSV

Lord, I am empty in myself, but You are the all-sufficient One. Thank You that You fill my heart and make me rich in Yourself.

December 24

Who can add to Christmas? The perfect motive is that God so loved the world. The perfect gift is that He gave His only Son. The only requirement is to believe in Him. The reward of faith is that you shall have everlasting life.

> You must understand that God has not sent his Son into the world to pass sentence upon it, but to save it—through him.

See John 3:17 Phillips

Lord, through Your Holy Spirit, help me to understand so much of the victory and joy of Your coming to earth that I enjoy Christmas more than ever before.

December 25

Happy Christmas! The shepherds told everyone what had happened. They heard the angels' message and they saw the newborn baby. What did they do? They told everyone! Let us do the same.

> And when they saw it they made known the saying which had been told them concerning this child; and all who heard it wondered at what the shepherds told them.
>
> Luke 2:17, 18 RSV

Father, You gave to shepherds the joy of being the first to worship Your Son on earth and tell the news of His birth. Thank You that we, too, may bring that very important message. It will honor Your name and save souls for eternity. What a joy!

December 26

If Jesus were born one thousand times in Bethlehem and not in me, then I would still be lost. There was no room in the inn for Him. Is there room in your heart for Him?

> Into my heart, into my heart,
> Come into my heart, Lord Jesus
> Come in today, come in to stay,
> Come into my heart, Lord Jesus.

> For God so loved the world that he gave his only Son. . . .
>
> John 3:16 RSV

Lord, teach my family and me to enjoy Christmas. Give me wisdom to organize my work and time in such a way that I find time to meditate on Your intense love, which You proved when you came to earth to die and rise again for the sins of the whole world. Help me to share this with the people around me.

December 27

Sometimes I do not feel as close to the Lord as before. I know who has moved. It is not the Lord but Corrie ten Boom. What do I do then? I tell Him who loves me. He forgives and cleanses me and then the fellowship is closer than ever.

> Stay always within the boundaries where God's love can reach and bless you.
>
> Jude 21 LB

Thank You, Lord, that I know You are with me. I claim Your promise, "I am with you always."

December 28

In Revelation 22 it is written that His servants shall serve Him. That means that heaven is a place of service. When we belong to Jesus we are citizens of heaven, and our outlook goes beyond this world. What a joy that our service will continue.

> Afraid of what?
> To enter into Heaven's rest
> And yet to serve the Master blessed,
> From service good to service best,
> Afraid of that?

> ... for the Lord God will be their light, and they shall reign for ever and ever.
>
> Revelation 22:5 RSV

Thank You, Lord, for the encouragement You give by telling us again and again that the best is yet to be.

December 29

A brother in Christ who experienced all the catastrophes which are mentioned here wrote me: "Although the dollar shall lose its value because of inflation; although my boat was destroyed by a hurricane; my trailer torn to pieces by a tornado; bombs fall in airports and theaters; no place in the world is safe: I will rejoice in the Lord, I will joy in the God of my salvation."

> Though the fig tree do not blossom, nor fruit be on the vines, the produce of the olive fail and the fields yield no food, the flock be cut off from the fold and there be no herd in the stalls, yet I will . . . joy in the God of my salvation.
> Habakkuk 3:17, 18 RSV

Thank You, Lord, that even when the worst happens in the life of the child of God, the best remains. Thank You that everything that happens fits into a pattern for good for those who love You.

December 30

Think of stepping on shore and finding it heaven; taking hold of a hand and finding it God's; breathing new air and finding it celestial; feeling invigorated and finding it immortality; of passing through a tempest to a new and unknown ground; of waking up well and happy and finding it Home.

> But, as it is written, "What no eye has seen, nor ear heard, nor the heart of man conceived, what God has prepared for those who love him."
> 1 Corinthians 2:9 RSV

Lord, thank You that You have given us, Your children, eternal life here and now, and that we know that unspeakable joy is awaiting us.

December 31

We have met for 366 days. On the last day of the year let us read what God's Word says in Philippians 3:13, 14 RSV and 1 Thessalonians 5:23 RSV:

Brethren, I do not consider that I have made it my own; but one thing I do, forgetting what lies behind and straining forward to what lies ahead, I press on toward the goal for the prize of the upward call of God in Christ Jesus.

May the God of peace himself sanctify you wholly; and may your spirit and soul and body be kept sound and blameless at the coming of our Lord Jesus Christ.

Jesus was Victor;
Jesus is Victor;
Jesus will be Victor. Hallelujah!

You may write to Corrie ten Boom at Box 2040, Orange, CA 92669. Her magazine THE HIDING PLACE is published quarterly from the same address.

Other Books by Corrie ten Boom

THE HIDING PLACE by Corrie ten Boom
The exciting true story of Corrie ten Boom and her
family, imprisoned for hiding Jews from the Nazis.
Cloth, HID, $6.95; Paper, HID-PA, $2.95

TRAMP FOR THE LORD by Corrie ten Boom
The remarkable 81-year-old Corrie shares with the
reader her experiences while traveling around the world
since her release from a World War II prison camp.
Cloth, R-TMP, $5.95; Paper, S-373, $2.95

IN MY FATHER'S HOUSE by Corrie ten Boom
The heartwarming account of the earlier part of Corrie's
life—the years before ''The Hiding Place.''
Cloth, RFH, $6.95

AMAZING LOVE	CTB-1, $1.25
A PRISONER AND YET	CTB-2, $1.25
DEFEATED ENEMIES	CTB-3, $ .35
MARCHING ORDERS FOR THE END BATTLE	CTB-4, $1.00
NOT GOOD IF DETACHED	CTB-5, $1.25
PLENTY FOR EVERYONE	CTB-6, $1.25
COMMON SENSE NOT NEEDED	CTB-7, $ .35

THESE BOOKS ARE AVAILABLE FROM YOUR
LOCAL CHRISTIAN BOOKSTORE OR BY MAIL
FROM: GRASON
              1303 Hennepin Avenue
              Minneapolis, Minnesota 55403

(Please enclose $.50 for postage with your order.)